ANTONIO MELI

Closing the Distance

How Emotional Connection Fills the Space Between Us

**HELD
TOGETHER**

PUBLISHING

Library of Congress Case
Meli, Antonio
Closing the Distance -How Emotional Connection Fills the Space Between Us
Case Number: 2025910896

First edition

ISBN: 979-8-9990151-0-5

Cover art by Wyatt Charron

This book was professionally typeset on Reedsy.
Find out more at reedsy.com

For the reader,
If you've ever sat across from silence and wondered if someone would stay,
this book is my way of saying yes.

Contents

Introduction

This book is not meant to be rushed.

It is not a story with a single arc, or a set of steps to follow.

It is a map of moments, emotional, relational, physical, that unfold in quiet ways.

You are invited to read this slowly.

To pause when a sentence echoes.

To reread lines that linger.

To mark the pages where something feels familiar.

Closing the Distance is organized by experience, not by plot. Each chapter explores a different layer of what it means to come closer, to yourself, to another person, to the spaces in between. Some chapters will feel like home. Others may feel like memory. A few may feel like hope, or grief, or longing in its rawest form.

You don't need to read it all at once.

You don't even need to read it in order.

But if you choose to go from start to finish, you'll notice a movement:

From the first glance, to the shared breath, to the silence, to the return.

From distance, to presence.

From fear, to trust.

From being across the room, to becoming part of the rhythm of someone's life.

Let this be a mirror, not a manual.

Let it sit with you.

Let it breathe.

And if at any point you feel seen, even just for a moment, then we've already come a little closer.

Chapter 1: Across the Room

We notice people before we know them.

Not through conversation or contact, but in the space they occupy, the way they sit, where their eyes fall, how their presence stirs the quiet air around them.

Across the room, someone exists in your line of sight like a possibility not yet named. There is no interaction, not yet. Just the awareness of them. A silent knowing that someone else is here.

Maybe you watch them laugh at something you didn't hear, or glance at their hands while they wait, still and folded. Your brain registers posture before personality, shape before story. They're just another body among many. But something about the way they are, it makes you feel aware in a different way.

We don't often talk about this first phase of connection. The moment before the moment. That pause before approach.

It's not romantic or dramatic, it's subtle. Often missed. But it's real.

Because space, in its own way, holds meaning. The space between you and them. The absence of words. The geometry of noticing.

You stand by the wall. They sit near the window. The room is crowded, but you aren't part of each other's world yet. And yet... part of you is already attuned. Already aware of their existence in the same square footage of air.

You observe. You don't mean to, but you do. Maybe they hold their cup in two hands instead of one. Maybe they lean forward when they read. Maybe they have a softness around the eyes that reminds you of something familiar.

There is no connection yet, only curiosity stretched thin across the invisible wires of awareness.

We often think of distance as what separates us. But distance can also be what protects us.

It gives us room to look before we leap. To consider before we commit.

From across the room, it's safe to wonder.

You don't have to perform. You don't have to risk rejection. There is no pressure in potential. Only space.

There's a kind of stillness in that. In the ability to observe without needing anything from the other person. No expectations. Just quiet attention.

It's in this gap that most relationships begin, not with touch or talk, but with a shift in awareness.

Think of how you've noticed someone before their name meant anything to you.

A classmate who sat diagonally across from you, always tapping their pencil.

A stranger in the waiting room who chose the seat facing the window.

A coworker you passed in the hall every day, nodding without speaking.

They lived in the periphery, not part of your story, not yet. But present.

And sometimes that presence changes something.

Maybe not all at once. But you begin to track them, subconsciously. When they enter a room, you notice. When they leave, something feels slightly less dense in the air.

The layout of a room matters more than we realize.

It defines the lines of possibility.

It governs who faces whom.

It shapes who we might brush past and who remains a distant figure.

Circular tables invite equality. Rows suggest hierarchy. An open floor draws connection; a corner, retreat.

We take mental notes without realizing it. How close is too close? Where do we sit if we don't want to be seen? What angle allows us to look without being caught looking?

Even our posture becomes part of the language. Legs crossed away or toward. Shoulders turned. Head tilted slightly.

And then there's eye contact, that invisible magnet. That terrifying risk. That hopeful thread.

Eye contact breaks the seal.

It changes distance from passive to active.

From across the room, it can feel like too much. Or everything.

A glance held half a second longer than it should be, enough to wonder if it meant something.

Enough to make you look again.

But not all distance is emotional. Sometimes the room is only a few steps wide, but it might as well be a mile.

You sit next to someone on the bus, your arms almost brushing, but you feel galaxies apart.

You're in the same kitchen, making coffee in silence, but your thoughts are light-years away from theirs.

You can hear their breathing, but not their heart.

Physical proximity doesn't always mean closeness.

And yet, distance can hold the weight of what's possible.

A safe zone before vulnerability.

A slow-burning pull before the leap.

Sometimes, we prefer distance.

It allows us to stay composed, unseen.

To remain the observer instead of the participant.

We admire from afar because it's easier than risking disappointment up close.

Because it's gentler to imagine someone than to learn they're not what we hoped.

But even then, something stirs. A question forms. A readiness begins to gather.

And in that readiness, we begin to shift, ever so slightly, toward the center of the room.

There's a hum in a room when you're aware of someone.

A quiet shift in atmosphere, almost nothing, almost everything.

You notice the way their foot taps beneath the table, or how they pause before speaking to someone else. You wonder what they sound like. What they think about when no one is talking to them. Whether they've noticed you noticing them.

That's the tension of the early distance. You don't know if anything is mutual, or if this feeling is only yours. But still, something in you watches.

You start mapping them in your internal landscape, the way you might mentally track a song that plays often in the background. Not always conscious, but present. Threaded into your awareness.

This space, this middle ground between anonymity and interaction, becomes a holding place for questions.

Would you even like them if you spoke?

Would they surprise you? Disappoint you?

Would something shift, forever, if one of you crossed the line?

Because that's what distance does: it creates the line.

The line between familiar and unknown. Between solitude and encounter. Between peace and risk.

Sometimes, we get comfortable in the watching.

Comfortable with the almost.

And there's a strange beauty in that.

Because from across the room, you get to imagine. You can make sense of them in your own way, free from contradiction or complexity. They are only what they appear to be. The way they hold themselves. The way they exist when they don't know you're looking.

It's safer that way.

There's no vulnerability in observation. No misunderstanding. No awkward silences or clumsy starts. Just the stillness of you, and the presence of them, separated by a room.

But comfort can also be a cage.

You may not be rejected, but you won't be known either.

And if you stay in that place too long, the room becomes a kind of purgatory. Suspended potential. Something that could have happened but never did.

The first step toward someone is rarely a physical one.

It begins in the mind.

The curiosity deepens. The wondering sharpens.

You start paying attention on purpose. You notice how they react when someone interrupts them. Whether they laugh easily or hold back. Whether they leave the room often or stay planted, quiet and watchful.

Their presence starts to inform your posture. Your attention. Your sense of gravity.

The room doesn't feel the same anymore. They've changed it, somehow.

And maybe you've changed too, just a little. Not because you've done anything, but because you're leaning, inward, slightly. Not yet forward, not yet toward. But inward. Toward some center you hadn't noticed until they walked in.

There's an art to being near someone without being with them.

A skill in navigating distance.

Maybe you take the seat closer to theirs, but not too close. Maybe you speak louder, hoping your voice carries. Maybe you linger in a doorway just a beat longer than needed, testing the current of connection without ever stepping fully in.

Every movement is coded with the same silent message:

I see you. Do you see me?

Still, nothing is said outright. Not yet.

You remain on opposite sides of the room. The air between you thick with unspoken possibility.

And the question begins to echo: What will it take to close the space?

The truth is, the space between people can be both honest and misleading.

It reveals interest and fear at the same time.

Some stand far back because they're uninterested. Others, because they care too much.

Distance can be apathy or restraint. Comfort or confusion. It takes time to tell the difference.

But space itself is not the enemy.

Space is a container. A stage. A holding pattern.

Within it, we build anticipation.

We watch and wait.

We allow the shape of connection to form on its own, without force.

And in that time, we learn.

We learn whether we're drawn in by who they are or just who we imagine them to be.

We learn if we're truly curious, or only infatuated with the mystery.

There's power in resisting the urge to fill the silence.

In letting the room remain wide.

In allowing the air to stretch between you, until the pull becomes undeniable.

This is not about games or hesitation. It's about honoring the space it takes to shift from noticing to knowing.

We all need a moment, a pause, to feel the contours of that pull.

Even when it's subtle.

Especially when it is.

Eventually, something does change.

A signal gets sent. A glance becomes a look.

And the stillness of distance begins to stir.

But this is where we stay for now.

Across the room.

Not touching. Not speaking.

Just existing, separately, but aware.

The beginning of all closeness lives here.

In this tension.

In this room.

In the moment before the moment begins.

We live in a world that moves quickly. We're trained to speak, respond, step forward, fill the gaps. Silence is often treated like a problem to solve, and distance, a failure to act.

But sometimes, there's wisdom in the waiting.

From across the room, you get time to observe without expectation. Time to watch a person unfold without the pressure to define them. You begin to notice things others overlook, the way someone folds their napkin, the pattern in their nervous fidgeting, how they watch other people speak before joining in.

That kind of noticing builds slowly, but it builds deeply.

It's not about romance. It's not even always about connection.

It's about presence.

About the way we begin to understand each other before words are exchanged.

When you pay attention from a distance, you're seeing someone in the unguarded moments, before they know they're being seen. It's raw. Subtle. More honest than we often realize.

And it's the birthplace of empathy.

Not in knowing someone's story, but in recognizing that they have one.

The room becomes a map. You begin to mark their movements. You track patterns, even without meaning to. They tend to stand near the bookshelf. They often check their phone but never type on it. They laugh when others do, but never start the joke.

These aren't facts. They're impressions.

And impressions are how we begin to form emotional coordinates.

That's the thing about this stage. It's more internal than shared.

You haven't built a connection, you've built a readiness for one.

There's a quiet shift in your posture, the way your attention sharpens when they enter. The room tilts, slightly. You notice.

It matters. That noticing. It's what turns space into something personal.

And yet, you don't move. Not yet.

Sometimes the distance feels safer. Sometimes it doesn't feel like your turn. Sometimes it's hard to tell whether what you feel is real, or just a flicker of interest in an otherwise ordinary day.

Still, it lingers.

They move a certain way and your thoughts catch. You imagine what it would feel like to say hello. You wonder if they'd smile, or seem surprised, or confused. The fear of misreading can be paralyzing.

What if the connection only exists in your mind?

What if they haven't noticed you at all?

This fear, the fear of assumption, is what keeps many people rooted in place.

Across the room, watching.

Alive with curiosity, frozen in uncertainty.

But even that has its own kind of value.

Sometimes, the distance helps you clarify what you want, not just from them, but from connection itself.

Are you drawn to the idea of them, or the reality?

Are you ready for the mess of closeness, or do you just crave the neatness of admiration?

Distance asks us questions that proximity can't.

Because when someone is still a mystery, they're a mirror too.

You see your own hopes reflected in them. Your own need to be seen. Your own readiness to be known.

Think about all the people who were once across the room from you.

People who were strangers until they weren't.

People you once saw and wondered about.

You probably don't remember the moment you met most of them.

But maybe you remember the moment before.

The glance. The silence. The presence.

That's where it starts.

The connections that shape us, the ones that change us, don't always arrive with fanfare.

Sometimes they begin in the quiet. In the space between.

In the feeling that someone matters, before you even know why.

Not all distance is meant to be closed.

Some people are simply meant to be witnessed.

To be admired, briefly, from afar.

They pass through the room and leave a mark, not because they became part of your life, but because they reminded you of something important.

Like the fact that you can still be moved.

Still be drawn.

Still feel the ache of possibility.

That's not nothing.

To feel that ache is to remember you're alive.

That your heart is still listening.

That the world is full of strangers who might not stay strangers.

There's something deeply human about the moment before closeness.

It's rich with contrast, stillness and tension, safety and risk, silence and anticipation.

And no matter how many times you've felt it before, it always arrives with a certain weight. Because it means something might begin. Something real.

But here's the truth: nothing happens without a shift.

At some point, the space between either expands or contracts.

The room doesn't stay suspended forever.

You either walk away, carrying only the imprint of that almost, or you move closer. You speak. You change the shape of the room by changing your place in it.

But before that moment comes, there's this one.

This in-between.

This strange, gentle ache that lives in the distance.

And maybe that's where much of our emotional life happens.

Not in the having, but in the hoping.

Not in the closeness, but in the pull toward it.

There are rooms you never forget.

Not because of what happened in them, but because of what almost did.

Because of who was there, and how the air felt charged with a presence you couldn't name.

Maybe it was a library or a living room, a train station or a crowded café. The details fade, but the feeling doesn't.

You remember scanning the space, and then stopping.

Not because something dramatic caught your eye, but because someone did, effortlessly, subtly. They were part of the setting until they weren't. Until they became the focus.

And still, you said nothing.

You didn't cross the room.

You didn't change your day.

You just noticed.

That noticing was enough to make the ordinary unforgettable.

It's strange how distance makes someone larger.

From far away, people seem taller, more mysterious. They carry more weight than they do up close. Not physically, but emotionally. Their outlines seem sharper, their gestures more meaningful.

Because you're not just seeing the person, you're seeing the possibility of them.

And possibility always casts a bigger shadow than reality.

You might later learn that they're shy or bold, soft-spoken or loud, warm or indifferent. But before all that, they're just a shape in the room. A presence that caught your attention. A person whose proximity is felt even when it isn't near.

From across the room, you give them a kind of reverence, not because they've earned it, but because your imagination fills in what you don't know.

That's the thing about space. It invites projection.

We don't just observe others. We build stories around them.

Maybe they remind you of someone you used to know.

Or someone you still hope to meet.

Or some part of yourself you thought you had outgrown.

We don't always fall in love with people.

Sometimes we fall in love with symbols.

With who someone represents to us before they even speak.

Across the room, that illusion can live without interference.

Without contradiction.

Without complexity.

It's both the gift and the limitation of distance.

It lets us imagine freely, but it also keeps us from seeing clearly.

At some point, clarity demands closeness.

And closeness demands courage.

But for now, in this moment, imagination feels easier.

You don't always know why a person stands out.

They might not be the most beautiful or the most charismatic. They might not speak loudly or move often. But something about them feels weighted. Charged. Important, somehow.

Maybe it's because they're not trying.

Maybe it's because their attention is elsewhere.

Maybe it's because, for the first time in a while, you've slowed down enough to feel your own attention shifting.

You watch the way they listen. The way they pause before replying to someone else.

You start to guess their thoughts.

You wonder what their voice would sound like saying your name.

It's silly, almost. You know that. But the mind wanders where it wants to, and in these moments, it chooses them.

Time stretches when you're watching someone you don't know.

A few seconds can feel like a full chapter.

The tilt of a head, the shift of a shoulder, the way their fingers rest on the edge of a table, everything is exaggerated by the tension of possibility.

This isn't obsession. It's attention, lit up.

It's what happens when a quiet part of you wakes up and asks,

Could this be something?

Even if you never speak.

Even if they leave before you move.

Even if this moment fades back into silence.

There was something. A thread. A spark.

Not yet a flame, but not nothing either.

And that's enough to make you feel a little more alive than you were the minute before.

It's easy to think these moments don't matter.

That if nothing happens, it wasn't real.

But that's not true.

The beginning of closeness isn't always dramatic.

Sometimes, it's just a shift inside you.

You saw someone.

You felt something.

You paused.

You let the world slow down for a beat and made space, not for them, exactly, but for what they represented.

That counts.

It matters that you're still capable of being moved.

In a way, we're always across the room from someone.

Even in relationships, even with people we love.

There are corners of another person we'll never fully reach.

Parts of them we only glimpse, half-lit, across some kind of internal space.

That's not failure. That's humanity.

No two people ever fully dissolve the space between them.

We all carry our own rooms inside us.

And closeness isn't about collapsing them, it's about finding the doorways.

From across the room, we get our first sense of those doorways.

We notice. We wonder. We begin to lean.

Not physically, not always.

But emotionally.

Quietly.

And that leaning is the first movement toward connection.

Noticing someone is one thing.

Letting that noticing change you is another.

It begins quietly. A single glance can become a habit. A moment of attention turns into anticipation. You start expecting them. Not overtly, not even intentionally, but you find yourself looking toward the doorway when you hear it open. You scan the space differently, hoping they're in it.

You don't call it anything yet. You're not sure it *is* anything. But you feel it. That low, steady hum beneath the surface of your routine.

They've taken up residence in your awareness.

And that matters, not because they're everything, but because your mind made room.

There's a language to distance. One most people never fully learn.

It's in how we move around each other without making contact.

How we share air but not words.

How we sense the shape of another person's presence without needing to interrupt it.

There's a kind of grace in that.

Letting someone exist without trying to capture them.

Letting yourself be drawn without acting on it right away.

You're watching. You're feeling. You're beginning to understand the rhythms of emotional gravity.

It's not always loud. It's not always romantic. Sometimes it's just *there*, the slow realization that someone affects the way you inhabit space.

That's enough to shift something in you.

People don't always realize how much of closeness is shaped before a single word is spoken.

The preparation happens internally. Quietly. Like drawing breath before singing. Like lifting your hand before a wave.

You're gathering something.

You're bracing, gently.

You're allowing the possibility to live in you before it ever lives between you.

And that takes trust, not in the other person, but in yourself.

In your ability to be affected.

In your willingness to be open to what might never come.

That trust is the first form of intimacy.

Before the conversation.

Before the moment shifts.

Before the room closes in around the two of you instead of keeping you apart.

You begin to wonder what their presence means to you.

You can't call it attraction, not quite. Not yet.

It's something subtler than that. More curious than clear.

It's the way their silence feels louder than other people's words.

The way your focus narrows slightly when they move.

The way your internal monologue adjusts to account for them, even when you don't mean to.

Maybe it's connection.

Maybe it's memory.

Maybe it's simply the moment asking you to pay attention.

But whatever it is, you're in it now.

The room has changed, and so have you.

You might replay certain moments in your head:

The first time they glanced in your direction.

The way they reached for something.

A half-smile that might not have been for you, but still felt like it landed.

These fragments become part of your day.

Little bookmarks of meaning.

Tiny confirmations that something's alive, even if it doesn't have a name yet.

That's the power of early awareness.

It magnifies everything.

Because your mind is scanning for clues.

Looking for openings.

Testing the air.

You are both grounded and drifting. Anchored by attention, but loosened by uncertainty.

And somehow, it feels good to float.

It's strange to care about someone you don't know.

Stranger still to feel like they've already left a mark.

You wouldn't be able to explain it to anyone else, not without sounding dramatic or delusional.

But inside, it's real. It's textured. It's yours.

And that's enough.

Some of the most important people in our lives start as feelings, not facts.

As curiosities. As presences.

You may not know what they're like when they're tired, or what stories they carry, or what makes them close off, but you know how they made you feel when you first saw them.

And that feeling can shape everything that comes after.

Eventually, the room begins to press in.

Not with urgency, but with invitation.

The space between starts to feel less like a buffer and more like a question.

How long can you stay here?

How long can this distance hold the weight of what's forming?

It's not a demand. It's a whisper.

A feeling that maybe, just maybe, you're ready to change positions.

To move from the corner of the room to the center.

To turn observation into interaction.

You still don't know what will happen.

You don't even know what you hope will happen.

But something in you is no longer content to stand still.

This is the last moment before the shift.

The breath before the word.

The stillness before the step.

There's nothing to prove.

No strategy to play.

Just you, holding the awareness of someone else.

Letting it fill you.

Letting it stretch you.

Letting it remind you that being human is, at its core, a reaching.

Across rooms.

Across silence.

Across the vast, invisible spaces between lives.

And what a gift it is, to feel that reach begin.

Some rooms stay with you, not for what was said or done, but for what was felt.

The quiet ache of wanting to speak.

The almost-step you never took.

The weight of noticing someone who might never know they were seen.

These are not regrets. They're remnants.

Proof that something moved in you, that your inner world responded, even when the outer one didn't.

Across the room, we learn the art of waiting.

Not passively, but attentively.

Not because we're unsure, but because something about the moment asks for stillness first.

We wait for the signal. The shift. The click in the atmosphere that tells us it's time to move.

And sometimes, it doesn't come.

Sometimes, the person leaves before you gather the courage.

Sometimes, the tension evaporates and the ordinary takes over again.

Sometimes, they were never meant to be more than a reminder, that you're still paying attention. That you still care. That your heart, even after all this time, is still capable of wonder.

We don't talk enough about how brave it is just to notice someone.

To let yourself be affected.

In a world full of distraction, choosing to pay attention is an act of presence.

It means you're willing to be disrupted, even slightly.

To let another person change the landscape of your inner space.

That's not small.

It's the beginning of every story, whether it grows or not.

There's a paradox in this kind of moment.

You feel closer to someone you've never touched than you sometimes do to people who are inches away.

Because emotional presence doesn't always follow physical rules.

It bends around silence. It stretches across space.

And when it's real, even the briefest moment can feel full, like the room itself is holding its breath.

You lock eyes across the floor. You recognize a rhythm in their stillness. You feel something without needing to define it.

This is not the climax. It's not even the inciting action.

But it's the beginning.

And beginnings have gravity.

Eventually, all noticing reaches a crossroads.

You either stay where you are and let the moment pass,

or you shift, just a little, into the next phase.

That shift might be a word. A glance held longer than usual.

A movement that brings your path slightly closer to theirs.

Sometimes they notice too.

Sometimes they don't.

Sometimes the moment fades without consequence.

But you felt it.

And that's enough to leave an imprint.

You may not cross the room today.

You may not ever.

But the room is no longer neutral.

It's become charged. A place where attention lived.

Where something subtle but meaningful took place.

This shift, from watching to wondering, from distance to desire, is the first step in closing the distance.

Even if no words are spoken.

Even if nothing ever happens.

Because you felt it.

The pull.

The spark of potential.

The awareness of someone else's existence, brightening the edges of your own.

That's where every connection starts.

Not with a touch.

Not with a name.

But with the feeling that someone is no longer just a stranger in a room.

The next chapters of closeness begin with that spark.

With the body leaning.

With the voice preparing to speak.

With the heart steadying itself against the unknown.

But all of it starts here.

With distance.

With quiet.

With the almost.

And with you, standing across the room, awake to the possibility of more.

Chapter 2: The Spark Between

There's a moment, brief and quiet, when something changes.

It might begin with a glance that lingers half a second longer than it should.

A word spoken softly but aimed precisely.

A coincidence that makes you laugh, because it feels too perfect to be random.

And suddenly, the space between you and another person isn't just space anymore.

It's possibility.

It's tension.

It's alive.

You feel it before you name it.

Before you understand what's happening, your body already knows.

The eyes return more quickly.

The chest opens without meaning to.

You lean, slightly, not forward, not obviously, but inward.

Something in you is beginning to turn.

That's the moment this chapter begins.

Not with action, but with attention.

Noticing was passive.

This is different.

This is when your attention becomes specific.

When you begin to track someone not just because they're there, but because *you care that they are.*

Curiosity reshapes everything.

Where before there was distance, now there's direction.

Where before there was background noise, now there's signal.

You want to understand them, how they think, what they notice, how they move through the world.

And in that wanting, something shifts in you.

You don't always realize it right away.

Sometimes it feels like nothing.

Just a glance.

Just a shared smile.

Just a line in a conversation that echoes later when you're alone.

But that's how sparks work.

They're small. Fleeting.

Easy to miss, and impossible to forget.

A spark doesn't light up the room.

It lights up *you*.

It sharpens your awareness.

It nudges your thoughts.

It makes the moment feel charged, even if nothing has changed outwardly.

Except something has.

You've started to feel the pull.

This shift can happen anywhere.

At a bus stop, waiting for the same ride.

In the breakroom, laughing at the same joke.

On a walk, reaching for the same door.

The context doesn't matter. The story is always the same.

Something ordinary becomes a little more vivid.

Someone expected becomes unexpectedly present.

And suddenly, you find yourself choosing proximity.

You sit nearer.

You speak more often.

You begin asking questions, not to fill the air, but to know them better.

Conversation becomes its own kind of nearness.

That's the magic of the spark.

It doesn't ask for commitment.

It doesn't demand clarity.

It simply invites you to notice more deeply.

You start to wonder about them when they're not around.

Not in a dramatic way, just in small, wandering thoughts.

You remember the way they laughed at something you said.

The pause before they answered your question.

The way they seemed to be holding back something, or maybe holding something in.

Your mind revisits these fragments, trying to piece together the bigger picture.

Because something in you wants to know more.

This isn't about falling in love.

It's about falling into interest.

About the shift from general to particular.

From "someone" to *this* one.

The room may still be full, but your focus isn't.

You've chosen a subject, whether or not you admit it.

And that choice, quiet, invisible, changes your orbit.

You start moving toward them, not necessarily with your feet, but with your attention.

You listen more closely when they speak.

You smile more easily when they're near.

You've begun to lean.

This is the middle ground between watching and reaching.

You haven't asked for anything yet.

You haven't risked anything yet.

But you're thinking about it.

You're considering what it would take to step closer.

To move from spark to flame.

To test the air between you and see if it carries the same weight for them.

It's a hopeful kind of uncertainty.

Not yet a risk.

But no longer safe.

You've felt something, and now you can't unfeel it.

In many ways, the spark is a mirror.

It shows you where you're open.

What you're longing for.

What you're willing to notice and be changed by.

It's not always about the other person.

Sometimes it's about what they awaken in you.

The part of you that wants to connect.

That's ready to see and be seen.

That's willing to step out of observation and into participation.

The spark asks a simple question:

Are you ready to come closer?

Not just to them, but to yourself.

There's a distinct difference between being in a room *with* someone and having them be *in the room* with you.

The first is physical.

The second is felt.

Before the spark, they were just part of the background. Another face, another presence, another person you might have passed a dozen times without thinking twice.

But now?

Now they pull your attention in like gravity.

You don't need to speak to know they're near. You feel it. Something inside orients itself toward them. Your awareness adjusts like your eyes do in changing light, subtle, automatic, but undeniable.

They're not just a person anymore.

They're *this person*. The one who matters now, for reasons you're still learning.

It happens so gently.

You hear them speak to someone else and catch yourself smiling.

You notice their shoes, their hands, the way they gesture when excited.

You start finding excuses to be nearby, not too close, not obvious, but close enough to be included if conversation happens to open.

And sometimes it does.

It starts with a question. A shared comment. A moment of overlap in an otherwise separate day.

You respond. They respond. And suddenly there's a bridge forming between you, narrow and new, but real.

The first words exchanged are rarely extraordinary. But they don't have to be.

It's not about what's said.

It's about the fact that it was said *to each other*.

That someone who was once across the room is now standing beside you, and the air between you carries not silence, but attention.

Sparks don't always burst. Sometimes they simmer.

There are connections that unfold in slow motion, where each interaction builds gently on the last, like notes in a melody you're just beginning to recognize.

You start to listen more deeply. You start to speak more freely.

You learn their cadence, the pauses in their rhythm, the things they find funny.

And something in you begins to soften.

You're not just intrigued anymore.

You're invested.

Even if only slightly, even if only silently.

And that investment changes how you move.

You start showing up a little differently, a little more tuned in, a little more available.

Your posture shifts.

Your eyes follow.

Your attention becomes a thread that keeps tugging.

Sometimes the spark comes in the form of timing.

A shared glance when the room gets quiet.

A knowing look when something strange happens.

A question you both think of at the same time.

These are the coincidences that feel like more than chance.

You know, logically, that anyone else could have been there.

But they weren't.

They were.

And that changes the shape of the memory.

The moment becomes marked not by what happened, but by who it happened with.

The room is no longer just a space.

It's a stage.

And proximity has become choreography.

You notice where they sit.

You calculate the path between you.

You sense the opportunities to engage, to remain, to return.

But it's more than logistics.

There's emotion in it.

A quiet hope. A flicker of anticipation.

You want to be near not just because of attraction, but because something in you feels steadier when they're around.

Like the edges of your day smooth out just a little.

Like the world makes slightly more sense when they're part of it.

The spark doesn't require reciprocation to exist.

It only needs your awareness.

Your shift.

Your movement toward.

But when it *is* returned, even slightly, the room tilts.

Suddenly the space between you shortens, not by feet or inches, but by feeling.

A look held just a bit longer.

A smile sent just for you.

The way their voice changes when it's you they're answering.

These are the signs that maybe, just maybe, they feel it too.

And that mutual awareness is electric.

Not loud, not explosive. But charged.

Like static in the air before a storm.

Something's coming.

You don't know what, but you feel it.

You begin to wonder where this is going.

You play out conversations in your head.

You remember small details and revisit them like favorite songs.

They said they liked quiet mornings.

They mentioned a sibling, a city, a dream.

They laughed at your joke, or maybe they laughed with you.

Every piece feels like a step, and you're counting them even if you pretend not to be.

Because you care.

Because you're hoping.

Because something in you wants to see what could happen *if*.

If they feel it too.

If the moment opens wider.

If you both keep showing up this way, leaning in, little by little, without ever naming it.

There's a kind of magic in the moments before definition.

Before you call it friendship.

Before you call it attraction.

Before you even know what it is.

There's only the feeling.

And feelings, when fresh, are tender things.

You don't want to overexpose them.

You don't want to break the spell by rushing to understand it.

So you savor the space.

You let it breathe.

You stay close, but not too close.

You listen for cues, and offer your own.

The spark becomes something you tend to, gently, carefully.

Not a fire yet. Not a commitment. But real.

And maybe, just maybe, enough.

Sparks are fragile.

Not because they're weak, but because they live in the space between certainty and unknown.

They are made of potential, and potential is always vulnerable.

You begin to realize how much you don't know.

What they're thinking.

How they're feeling.

Whether they noticed that lingering glance as deeply as you did.

And in that not-knowing, your imagination starts to work overtime.

You analyze tone. You scan body language. You replay moments not because you're unsure they happened, but because you're trying to make sense of what they meant.

This is the part where closeness still feels like a question.

A beautiful one.

But a question, all the same.

You catch yourself hesitating.

Should you say something more direct?

Should you let the moment breathe?

Is it too soon to be this aware of someone?

Is it too much to hope they're aware of you, too?

The spark brings joy, yes, but it also brings risk.

The risk of misreading.

The risk of moving too fast, or too slow.

The risk of caring before they do.

And yet, you keep leaning in.

Not because you're certain.

But because something in you wants to know.

Wants to explore what this could become, not in grand gestures, but in small, steady presence.

This is where emotional attention becomes directional.

You're no longer just noticing. You're responding.

Your thoughts orbit around them more freely.

Your questions carry intention.

Your presence starts to hold weight, even if you don't speak.

You become aware of yourself in relation to them, how you act, how you appear, how your energy lands.

You check your words more carefully.

You listen more fully.

You offer pieces of yourself in ways that feel subtle but sincere.

Because something about this person makes you want to be known.

Makes you want to reach across the quiet, just a little more.

The spark creates movement.

Emotional, yes, but also physical.

You begin to shift your body without thinking.

You face toward them when they enter a space.

You adjust your chair to include them in the circle.

You pause when they speak, not just to hear, but to show that you're listening.

Even your stillness becomes intentional.

You're not performing. You're not pretending.

You're *present*, more than you usually are, even in familiar rooms.

And they bring that out of you.

Or maybe the possibility of them does.

Either way, something's different now.

Sometimes, the most powerful connections begin in silence.

Before the conversations get deep.

Before the vulnerability gets spoken.

Before the names become central to your day.

They begin in the way you start moving in response to someone else's gravity.

And that's what the spark really is:

An internal reorientation.

Your emotional compass turns, however slightly.

Your energy begins to tune itself to theirs.

Your awareness expands to make space for a new orbit.

That shift doesn't require agreement.

It doesn't need to be mutual, though it's magic when it is.

All it requires is honesty.

With yourself. With your intention. With what you're beginning to feel.

Of course, doubt visits too.

You wonder if you're imagining things.

If you're reading into kindness.

If you're attaching meaning to gestures that are simply polite.

It's a natural instinct, to protect yourself from disappointment.

To remind your heart that it's safer not to assume.

That not all attention is interest.

That not all sparks catch.

But protection and connection rarely live in the same room.

You can't insulate yourself and reach out at the same time.

And so you live in the tension, the pull between hope and hesitation.

The spark lives there too.

There's a quiet bravery in continuing to show up.

To keep bringing your presence.

To keep offering your attention.

To keep letting your interest live without needing it to be confirmed.

That kind of openness is rare.

Not performative. Not dramatic.

Just steady.

You don't demand closeness.

You create the conditions for it.

You allow them to respond, or not.

To meet you halfway, or not.

To notice you, or not.

And even if they don't, even if this spark stays only with you, you've still grown from it.

Because something in you was lit.

And light, once sparked, always finds somewhere to go.

You begin to notice the way you feel around them.

Not just what they do, but what *you* do, when they're near.

Are you softer?

More attentive?

More grounded?

Do they bring out curiosity in you, or caution?

Do you feel drawn to speak, or comfortable in the quiet?

The answers don't have to be clear. But the noticing matters.

Because connection isn't just about being with someone.

It's about who you become when you are.

And the spark is the first sign of that becoming.

If you're lucky, they'll notice too.

Not the full depth of what you feel, not right away, but enough to turn their attention in your direction.

Enough to meet you with the same pause.

The same stillness.

The same interest, waiting to unfold.

When two people feel the spark at the same time, something rare happens.

The room changes.

The space tightens.

Not physically, but emotionally.

It's no longer two people sharing a space.

It's two people sharing a center.

Everything else fades, if only for a moment.

And in that shared moment, you know.

This matters.

Whatever it is, however new, however uncertain, it matters.

You begin to understand how attention becomes connection.

It's not through one grand moment, but a string of small, near-invisible gestures.

The way you hold their gaze for a second longer.

The way they tilt their head when listening to you.

The way time bends slightly when you're speaking to each other, like the room continues on without you, but neither of you notice.

31

It's not about intensity. It's about clarity.

The feeling that this matters more than the rest.

And slowly, the spark becomes a language, one only the two of you are fluent in.

You speak more often now.

Not always about important things, but with more intention.

There's a rhythm forming. A conversational current that pulls you closer without force.

You begin to share more, not secrets, not yet, but small glimpses.

Stories, preferences, reactions.

Enough to reveal your shape.

And they respond, not just with words, but with attention.

They remember what you said last week.

They follow your train of thought when others don't.

They reference something small and personal, something you forgot you even told them.

And just like that, your presence is mirrored.

What you offered has returned.

The spark, once quiet, begins to warm.

It's in these early exchanges that emotional safety begins to form.

Not because you've known each other long.

Not because everything is understood.

But because something about your attention feels mutual.

There's a respect to it. A listening.

A sense that even in this early phase, you are being held with care.

That kind of feeling is rare.

Not manufactured. Not promised.

Just offered, naturally, consistently.

And you start to relax.

Not all at once. Not entirely.

But your shoulders drop.

Your laughter comes easier.

Your guard, slightly, lowers.

That's how the distance begins to dissolve.

You're still not close, not fully.

But you're not far anymore either.

There's a nearness now that isn't just spatial.

It's emotional. Intentional.

You find yourself looking for their presence in the room, not because you're unsure if they're there, but because their presence orients you.

You start to notice absence as much as presence.

The empty chair. The missed conversation.

The small disappointment when you realize today won't carry their voice.

And in that noticing, you recognize what's forming.

It's not love.

It's not dependence.

It's simply awareness deepening into care.

Not all sparks grow. Some fade.

But the ones that do grow, they do so with tenderness.

They're fed by consistency.

By showing up again and again.

By speaking even when it would be easier to stay silent.

By staying in the moment long enough for trust to root.

You don't have to know what it will become to know that it matters now.

This moment, this mutual spark, is its own kind of presence.

You don't need a label for it.

You don't need a future plan.

All you need is to honor the pull.

To be honest about what's stirring.

To keep following the thread that keeps tugging you toward each other.

At some point, the physical space begins to reflect the emotional shift.

You sit closer.

You walk together without needing to ask.

You stand beside each other like it's the most natural thing in the world.

And others might not notice.

Or they might.

Because something's changed, not dramatically, but undeniably.

There's an ease in your proximity.

An unspoken permission to be near.

That nearness doesn't demand anything.

It doesn't need to be loud.

It just is.

Like gravity. Like weather. Like something slowly becoming familiar.

You laugh more now.

Not because everything is funny, but because being seen makes things lighter.

Your conversations are still simple, but they carry weight.

You remember what they say.

They remember how you said it.

This is the beginning of knowing.

Not fully, not yet, but enough to start forming the shape of someone else in your mind.

And you realize: this is how closeness begins.

Not in declarations.

But in the accumulation of moments where you feel more yourself in someone else's presence.

The spark may have started the movement.

But now, the movement has its own momentum.

There's still room for uncertainty.

You don't know what this will become.

You're not sure how they'll feel next week, next month.

You don't even know how *you'll* feel.

But you're here.

You're noticing. You're engaging.

You're participating in something quietly unfolding.

And that's what matters.

That you showed up.

That you allowed the spark to guide you from stillness into motion.

From wondering to reaching.

From across the room... to side by side.

There's a moment, often unnoticed, where you realize you've stopped watching and started participating.

You're no longer just orbiting the same room.

You're in each other's space with purpose now, not constantly, but with intention.

You make eye contact more freely.

You ask deeper questions, even casually.

You remember small things: their favorite tea, the way they always say "right?" at the end of a thought, the pause before they share something personal.

You begin to build a rhythm.

Not a routine, exactly, but a pattern of mutual presence.

And that's what the spark has become, not just a flicker, but a rhythm.

It's still early.

You know that.

There are things you haven't said, stories you haven't told.

You haven't seen them in every season.

You don't know how they respond to stress, to silence, to distance.

But you've seen enough to keep showing up.

Enough to want more.

That wanting isn't heavy. It's light.

Gentle.

Something you carry in your chest like a quiet invitation: stay close.

You aren't rushing.

You don't need answers yet.

You're just beginning to feel the comfort of their nearness, not the dramatic kind, but the subtle, grounding kind.

You've noticed how being around them changes you.

You slow down. You pay attention.

You speak with more care, not out of fear, but out of respect.

You think about your words differently, not to impress, but to connect.

And they seem to respond in kind.

They lean in. They smile more easily.

They find ways to return your attention, even when the moment doesn't ask for it.

These are not grand gestures.

They are everyday moments colored by mutual presence.

And that's what makes them matter.

When you sit next to each other now, it feels natural.

You don't think about how it happened, you just end up near.

Your bodies find symmetry without effort.

Your voices carry toward each other like they're following a path already drawn.

You're not trying to control the outcome.

You're letting the current take you.

But even as you float, you're steering, ever so slightly, toward warmth.

There's still space between you.

But it's different now.

Not distance.

Just air.

And air can be crossed with a word, a look, a laugh.

You're not across the room anymore.

Sometimes the spark grows into something else.

Something steady.

Something shared.

Sometimes it doesn't.

Sometimes life pulls you apart before you get to know what it might have become.

But either way, the spark leaves something with you.

Not just a memory, but a mark.

Proof that you were open.

That you allowed yourself to lean toward someone without knowing how they'd respond.

That you risked your quiet to be part of something more.

And that's never wasted.

Because it shaped you.

Because it taught you how to feel again.

How to move.

How to open, just a little, in a world that often asks us to stay closed.

You won't always remember what you talked about.

But you'll remember how it felt when they turned toward you.

How the room softened.

How you felt more awake, more alive, just by being near them.

That kind of memory lingers.

It becomes part of your emotional muscle.

Something you carry forward into other rooms, other lives.

It reminds you that connection doesn't always require explanation.

That interest is its own form of intimacy.

That the moment you begin to care, something begins to grow.

Even if you never name it.

Even if it never becomes more.

The spark isn't a promise.

It's an opening.

It's not a destination.

It's a beginning.

It asks only one thing of you:

To notice.

To feel.

To respond, even just a little, with honesty.

Because honesty, at this stage, is everything.

Not a confession.

Not a declaration.

Just the quiet courage to show up with your attention intact.

To stay open long enough for something to become real.

And maybe that's what closeness always begins with.

Not proximity.

Not words.

But a shift.

An internal moment where you stop being alone in a room full of people. Where someone becomes distinct from the noise.

Where you begin to feel the line between your world and theirs blur, even slightly.

That's the spark.

And now that it's lit, the real story begins.

Chapter 3: Conversation as a Bridge

Closeness begins quietly.
But at some point, it speaks.
Not loudly. Not always with certainty.
But with words, careful, halting, hopeful.
Words that reach across the space between two people and ask,
Are you there? Are you listening? Can I meet you here?
Conversation is not just noise.
It's not just sound.
It's a thread.
A way of saying: I'm trying to build something.
A bridge from where I stand to where you are.
And with each sentence, we lay another piece.
There's a moment when silence becomes unbearable, not because it's empty,
but because it holds too much.
The unspoken interest.
The questions not yet asked.
The curiosity that can no longer sit quietly in the background.
So we speak.
Not with answers, but with attempts.
Not with certainty, but with courage.
Even a simple "hi" is a kind of offering.
A signal fire across the room.
A test balloon, rising to see if anyone reaches back.
When you first speak to someone you've noticed for a long time, it can feel

like tearing through glass.

The moment is fragile.

The stakes, strangely high.

You've imagined this person for days, maybe weeks.

You've constructed a quiet rhythm around their presence.

And now, you're inviting them to become real.

That's what conversation does.

It collapses the fantasy and opens the door to truth.

You hear their voice.

You see how they react.

You learn what surprises you, what draws you closer, what doesn't match the image you held.

But even when the illusion fades, the potential deepens.

Because now, you're not just watching.

You're participating.

Conversation is a brave act.

It reveals you.

Not all at once, but piece by piece.

Your tone.

Your timing.

The words you choose and the ones you avoid.

All of it adds up to a kind of map, a shape of who you are in that moment.

And if they respond with their own shape, something begins to build.

Not just a bridge.

But a rhythm.

Words aren't just tools for meaning.

They carry energy.

The way someone says your name.

The pauses between their thoughts.

The warmth or tension in their voice.

These subtleties matter more than the words themselves.

Because what we're really searching for isn't information.

It's resonance.

We want to feel that we're being met, not just heard.

That someone is leaning in, not just standing near.

Tone is often the first sign of emotional safety.

You can tell, almost instantly, whether someone is present, truly present, with you.

And when they are, your guard lowers.

Your voice softens.

Your body leans forward, not as strategy, but as instinct.

There's a difference between talking and connecting.

Talking is linear. Surface-level.

It moves from topic to topic like skipping stones across a lake.

Connection drops in deeper.

It lives in the places where silence isn't awkward.

Where your words don't need to be perfect.

Where the conversation bends toward vulnerability, not in dramatic confession, but in small, human truths.

"I didn't sleep well."

"I've been thinking about that too."

"I used to love that song."

Simple things. Real things.

They create openings.

They build trust.

They allow someone to know you not just as a performer, but as a person.

The bridge of conversation isn't built in one exchange.

It's built in return.

The willingness to keep showing up.

To keep asking, keep listening, keep offering something genuine.

Over time, these moments become a path, a soft, worn trail between two lives.

You remember their preferences.

They ask about your day.

You develop in-jokes, small references only the two of you understand.

Language becomes shorthand.

A way to say "I see you" without needing to explain how.
This is when the bridge becomes more than functional.
It becomes personal.
You start to notice how your body mirrors theirs.
How your speech patterns begin to align.
How your laughter overlaps without effort.
These are signs of closeness forming.
Not because you've planned it.
But because people naturally calibrate to the ones they care about.
We lean in.
We match tone.
We echo, gently, as a way of saying "me too."
Conversation becomes more than exchange.
It becomes attunement.
And that attunement is what draws us further in.
The first time someone really listens to you, truly listens, it's unforgettable.
They're not just waiting to speak.
They're not nodding out of politeness.
They're there. With you. Inside the moment.
Their attention doesn't drift.
Their eyes don't scan the room.
They stay where you are, not to fix, not to judge, just to *be* there.
That kind of listening is rare.
And when it happens, something shifts.
You feel seen.
Not for your performance, not for your usefulness, but for your presence.
And in return, you offer more.
Not to impress.
Just because you want to keep the bridge open.
That's how connection grows.
Not through perfectly chosen words.
But through presence.
Through willingness.

Through the soft, shared rhythm of give and receive.

You don't have to be brilliant.

You don't have to be eloquent.

You just have to be honest.

Even if that honesty shows up as hesitation.

Even if it takes the form of "I don't know what I'm trying to say."

Even if it means saying something awkward, unsure, or incomplete.

Because sincerity is more powerful than polish.

We don't bond through perfection.

We bond through being real.

Over time, conversation shifts shape.

It begins to hold more layers.

More nuance.

More weight.

You don't just talk about the day.

You talk about what the day felt like.

What it reminded you of.

Where it touched something deeper.

You start saying things like:

"I haven't told many people this."

"I'm not sure why I remember that."

"I didn't expect this to come up."

And the moment those words leave your mouth, the space between you changes.

The bridge isn't just functional now.

It's alive.

And it carries more than sound, it carries trust.

Not every conversation has to be deep.

But it's the *possibility* of depth that makes a connection feel safe.

The knowledge that if needed, the two of you *could* go there.

That if something hard came up, the bridge wouldn't break.

This is what builds emotional architecture.

Not how much is said, but how much space is made for what might be said.

You don't rush it.

You don't demand it.

You just leave the door open.

And sometimes, that's all someone needs to feel held.

You notice how your voice sounds different when you speak with them.

It's a little lighter.

Or steadier.

Or slower, in the best way, like you don't have to hurry.

There's no rush to explain yourself.

No pressure to be entertaining.

No fear of taking up too much room.

Because they're not just letting you talk, they're meeting you in the talking.

And you find yourself wanting to do the same.

You lean in.

You respond with care.

You hold their words like something worth protecting.

Even silence becomes meaningful.

Not awkward.

Not empty.

Just full, in a quiet, steady way.

A kind of mutual exhale.

That's when you know the bridge is real.

When the space between words still feels like connection.

When quiet doesn't disconnect you, it affirms that something true is already in place.

You sit together, saying nothing, and it says everything.

This doesn't mean you know everything about them.

Or that they know everything about you.

You don't need full understanding to feel close.

You just need resonance.

The sense that when you speak, something in them rings in response.

And when they speak, something in you settles.

That's what conversation at its best can do.

Not inform, but align.

You don't just hear each other.

You *feel* heard.

And that feeling builds something lasting.

Eventually, the bridge gets used for more than talking.

It becomes the path for comfort.

For support.

For the unspoken check-in.

They can tell when you're tired.

You can sense when they're off.

A small look, a soft "you okay?", and the weight begins to lift.

Because the connection isn't just verbal anymore.

It's emotional. Physical.

Lived-in.

You don't need full sentences to communicate.

You've built something that speaks in presence.

But it all began with words.

With a conversation.

With the courage to reach, not knowing if they would reach back.

That's the quiet bravery of connection.

It asks you to go first, or at least, to meet someone halfway.

To speak even when your voice shakes.

To ask even when you fear silence in return.

Every real relationship starts there.

On the edge of uncertainty.

With the simple, quiet risk of "Hi."

Conversation is often underestimated.

We treat it like filler, a way to pass time, to exchange details, to stay polite.

But when we let it, conversation becomes one of the most intimate acts available to us.

It is presence in motion.

It is vulnerability made audible.

It's not just about telling stories.

It's about revealing how you carry them.

The story of your morning.

The story of your scar.

The story behind the way you pause before answering certain questions.

All of it begins to form the outline of who you are, not just your facts, but your felt experience.

And slowly, you allow someone else to see that outline too.

Sometimes, it's what you don't say that builds the most trust.

The moment you hesitate.

The breath you take before answering.

The things you choose not to say, not because you're hiding, but because you're still holding them gently.

A good listener hears the edges of those silences.

They don't press.

They wait.

And in that waiting, you feel respected.

You feel free to offer your story at your own pace, to bring what's still soft into the open only when it's ready.

Conversation, at its best, is not a demand.

It's a shelter.

There's a rhythm to emotional dialogue.

Not just the exchange of thoughts, but the exchange of presence.

You begin to learn when to speak and when to stay quiet.

When to affirm, and when to just sit beside someone's truth.

You start to feel the unspoken layers:

What someone means beneath what they say.

The tension that rides under the joke.

The fear that shows up disguised as a smile.

These are the deeper frequencies of speech.

Not always visible.

But always felt.

And when someone meets you there, beneath the surface, something inside you exhales.

Because you don't have to explain it all.

You just have to be there, honestly.

When conversation becomes attuned, it becomes a kind of tether.

You start to notice how much someone's voice steadies you.

How their tone brings you back into your body.

How even short exchanges, a check-in, a shared look, remind you that you're not alone.

This is how emotional bridges grow stronger.

Not just through long talks, but through consistency.

Through showing up again and again.

Through treating each word like it matters, because it does.

People don't always remember what you said.

But they remember how it felt to speak with you.

And that feeling, over time, becomes the ground you both stand on.

You find yourself reaching out more.

Not because you need anything specific, but because you enjoy who you are when you're talking to them.

You feel seen.

You feel challenged.

You feel softened, in the best way.

And so the conversation extends, not just across rooms, but across days.

You send a message when something reminds you of them.

You wait for their reaction to a story you know they'll appreciate.

You ask questions, not just to know, but to care.

That's the real work of closeness.

Not constant contact.

But intentional contact.

A mutual willingness to keep the thread alive.

There are moments when conversation falters.

You misunderstand.

You say too much.

You say too little.

But even those moments have value.

Because connection doesn't require perfection, it requires repair.

You notice their silence and check in.

They notice your distance and stay present.

You come back. You clarify. You continue.

This is where trust takes root.

Not in never messing up, but in always returning.

Some conversations leave you feeling lighter.

Not because they solved anything.

But because you didn't have to carry it alone.

You said it out loud.

And someone held it.

And somehow, that was enough.

Other times, conversation uncovers something new.

A part of yourself you hadn't shared.

A dream you hadn't spoken.

A fear that found its first words.

And the person on the other end doesn't flinch.

They listen. They stay.

And in that moment, something grows, not just between you, but within you.

Because you realize: I can bring my whole self here.

And that is the beginning of belonging.

You begin to see the power of presence through words.

Not just what you say, but how you say it.

Not just how you speak, but how you receive.

The bridge you're building doesn't have guardrails.

It doesn't need them.

Because what holds it together isn't structure, it's attention.

Sincere, sustained, steady attention.

And that's rarer than we admit.

You don't need to speak constantly to maintain it.

Sometimes, the bridge is simply knowing that when you do reach out, even after hours, days, or longer, it will still hold.

That your words will still matter.

That your voice will still be met.

That's when you know connection has matured.

It no longer needs constant reinforcement.

It simply needs presence when it counts.

And when it counts, you show up.

So do they.

And that bridge, quietly built over time, becomes one of the most meaningful things you carry.

Conversation is a threshold.

It's the point where the internal becomes external.

Where what you think and feel begins to find shape in sound.

Sometimes, this shift is effortless, the words come naturally, like water from a steady stream.

Other times, it's clumsy.

You trip over what you're trying to say.

You second-guess whether it's the right time.

You question whether the other person is ready to receive it.

But the attempt still matters.

Because even the effort is a kind of intimacy.

It says: I'm willing to risk the mess to reach you.

Not every moment of closeness is built on profound statements.

Some of the deepest connection comes from saying things like:

"That reminds me of something."

"I forgot to tell you what happened today."

"Wait, can I ask you something random?"

These are the hinge points.

The small invitations.

The ordinary doors we open to let someone further in.

Because what we're really offering isn't content.

It's company.

We're not just telling stories.

We're saying, "Stay with me a little longer."

The bridge of conversation grows stronger the more it's used.

With each exchange, trust becomes layered.

You remember how they responded the last time you opened up.

You start to believe they'll handle your voice with care again.

And when that care proves consistent, when you are not only heard but welcomed, your words begin to carry less fear.

You speak more easily.

You ask questions without bracing for rejection.

You begin to tell the truth, not just the polished version.

Because now, it feels safe to do so.

At a certain point, words stop being just communication.

They become comfort.

A familiar phrase.

A particular way they say your name.

The sound of their laugh at the end of a sentence.

Even when you're apart, the memory of their voice lingers.

It becomes a kind of echo, a presence that stays with you long after the conversation ends.

And when you speak again, it's not starting from scratch.

It's continuing.

The bridge hasn't gone anywhere.

You just return to it.

And each time you do, it feels more like home.

Conversation also teaches pace.

You learn how to follow, how to lead, how to pause.

You sense when they need more time to answer.

You recognize when a story has meaning beneath the surface.

You learn to wait, without pushing, for the next part to come naturally.

And they do the same for you.

Together, you create a rhythm that honors both of your timing.

There's no rush.

No script.

No urgency to reach a destination.

Only the unfolding.

Only the trust that this space is worth returning to.

Sometimes, one sentence opens a door that can't be closed.

It might be:

"I've never told anyone this."

Or "Can I ask you something personal?"

Or "I don't know why I'm sharing this with you."

You feel the air shift.

You hear something delicate in their voice.

You realize that what they're saying could have been kept quiet, but it wasn't.

They chose to say it *here*.

To *you*.

And in that moment, you feel the weight of trust being handed over.

Not like a burden.

But like a gift.

One you carry carefully.

One that makes the bridge stronger just by being spoken across it.

The more you talk, the more you realize that closeness isn't made from big declarations.

It's made from small, repeated moments of honesty.

Not, "I love you," right away, but,

"I missed you."

"I kept thinking about what you said."

"I'm really glad we talked."

These are the bricks.

These are the beams.

This is the kind of conversation that doesn't just connect, it *constructs*.

Something new.

Something shared.

Something worth protecting.

Even disagreement, when handled with care, can deepen connection.

You won't always see things the same way.

You might say something that lands wrong.

You might be misunderstood.

But if the bridge is strong enough, you come back.

You clarify.

You listen more closely.

You try again.

This is where trust becomes resilience.

Where you realize that your bond isn't fragile, it's flexible.

It can bend.

It can hold weight.

It can carry tension without collapsing.

And that kind of bridge?

That's rare.

That's worth building.

Conversation is not just what happens between words.

It's what happens between hearts.

It is the slow, deliberate act of making yourself known,

and letting someone else do the same.

Not all at once.

Not forever guaranteed.

But moment by moment, showing up to speak and hear and respond.

It's in that simple act that so many lives begin to touch.

So many distances begin to close.

And so many bridges are quietly, steadily built.

There comes a moment in any growing connection where conversation is no longer just about discovery, it becomes something you return to. A place, almost. A shared space you build together and carry with you.

You don't always plan to talk.

You just do.

It happens naturally now, like breathing.

There's no need to think through every word.

You know they'll understand the tone, the shorthand, the pauses.

You've found a rhythm, and with it, a kind of ease.

The bridge isn't tentative anymore.

It's familiar.

It holds without needing to prove anything.

Even silence, now, is richer.

You can sit together in quiet and not feel pressure to fill it.

You know that silence isn't absence, it's permission.

To just be.

To just rest.

To just exist beside each other without the need to perform.

That's how you know the conversation has grown into something more.

Not every word is necessary, because the connection doesn't depend on speech.

The bridge holds, even in stillness.

You begin to realize how few people you've truly talked with, not just spoken to, but truly met in dialogue.

Where you weren't just exchanging facts or stories, but presence.

Where you weren't just listening to respond, but listening to feel.

Where you weren't just sharing updates, but opening a window into your interior life.

These conversations are rare.

Not because people don't want them, but because they're often too busy, too afraid, too distracted to stay long enough for them to unfold.

But here, with this person, you've stayed.

And they've stayed too.

And something meaningful has emerged from that staying.

You carry parts of their voice with you now.

You hear them in your head when you make a decision.

You picture how they'd respond to something funny.

You find yourself thinking, "I can't wait to tell them this."

This is how a bridge becomes a bond.

When they aren't just part of your conversations, they're part of your thinking.

And in some quiet, powerful way, part of your becoming.

Not every connection lasts.

Not every conversation turns into a relationship.

But every real exchange leaves a mark.

Because words matter.

Presence matters.

The effort to reach someone, and to let them reach you, matters.

Even brief conversations, when shared honestly, can echo for years.

A sentence you didn't expect.

A laugh that softened your day.

A simple truth spoken clearly.

These things become touchstones.

And sometimes, they're enough to change the direction of your story.

When you think back on the people who shaped you, it won't always be the ones who stayed the longest.

Sometimes it's the one who said the thing you needed to hear when you didn't know how to ask.

The one who asked a better question.

The one who looked you in the eyes and didn't look away.

Words don't need a long timeline to make a lasting impact.

They just need sincerity.

And timing.

And someone brave enough to say them out loud.

In the end, all conversation is a reaching.

A way of saying, "Here I am. Will you meet me here?"

It doesn't have to be poetic.

It doesn't have to be deep.

It just has to be true.

You don't always know what will come of it.

You don't always get to control the outcome.

But every time you choose to speak, with honesty, with kindness, with intention, you are building something.

A bridge.

A possibility.

A path toward closeness.

And even if the other person never walks across it, you've still done something quiet.

You've chosen connection over comfort.

You've offered yourself, even if just a little.

You've said: I'm here. I care. I want to know you.

And that is always a beautiful beginning.

Chapter 4: Side by Side

There's a quiet magic in walking beside someone.

Not talking, not touching, just moving in the same direction, together.

The world moves around you. Other people pass, sounds rise and fade, but your steps remain steady. In sync or not quite, it doesn't matter. You're both going somewhere, and for now, you're going there *with* each other.

This kind of closeness is soft.

It doesn't ask questions.

It doesn't need to be declared.

It simply exists, shoulder to shoulder, breath beside breath, two bodies aligned not by pressure but by choice.

There are different kinds of nearness.

Some are loud. Intense. Charged with emotion or urgency.

But this one, the kind where you sit beside someone, or move with them, or simply share space, this one is gentle.

It's the kind of closeness that doesn't ask for attention.

It doesn't pull or perform.

It just offers presence.

And in doing so, it gives permission for both people to simply *be*.

No pressure to maintain eye contact.

No need to fill the air with words.

Just existing near each other, letting silence do part of the talking.

This kind of physical alignment teaches you something important:

That not all connection needs intensity.

That nearness can be quiet.

That companionship is sometimes more powerful than conversation.

When you walk with someone, you begin to sense their rhythm.

How fast they move.

How they shift their weight.

When they slow down to match you, or speed up without thinking.

These are small, unnoticed gestures. But they reveal care.

A willingness to align.

To stay together, even in motion.

It's not just about where you're going.

It's about how you're getting there, and who you're getting there with.

Think of how many important moments in your life have happened beside someone, not in front of them.

Sitting together on a bench.

Driving in a car at night.

Walking through a city, shoulder to shoulder, talking about nothing and everything.

There's something about facing the same direction that allows us to open up more easily.

Maybe because there's less pressure to perform.

Maybe because we're not being watched, we're being accompanied.

And in that side-by-side movement, things begin to surface.

Stories. Memories. Questions that wouldn't have come out face to face.

Some truths only rise when you're not looking each other in the eye.

Shared direction creates emotional ease.

It sends a message: I'm with you, not against you.

We're moving forward, not confronting.

We're walking together, not interrogating each other.

This is where the pace of connection becomes visible.

You start to notice if one of you tends to rush.

If the other lingers, always looking around.

If you naturally find balance, or if you take turns slowing down.

It's not about who leads.

It's about how you adjust.

How you listen to each other's movement.

How you allow space without letting someone fall behind.

This is the work of closeness, not just sharing destination, but sharing pace.

There are moments when sitting beside someone feels more intimate than any embrace.

Because it holds the tension without trying to resolve it.

Because it says, "I'm here," without demanding, "Tell me everything."

Because it honors whatever the moment is, quiet or heavy or hopeful, with steady presence.

This is the difference between pressure and partnership.

Sometimes what we need most is not to be held tightly.

Just to be held near.

Not to be fixed.

Just to be accompanied.

You begin to notice the subtleties of comfort.

The way your arms rest without brushing.

The way your knees point in the same direction.

The way your breathing starts to match, even if your minds are miles apart.

This is when bodies speak without words.

When proximity becomes a kind of language.

It doesn't say, "I know what you're feeling."

It says, "You don't have to feel it alone."

And that difference, that slight, powerful difference, is what makes side-by-side connection feel safe.

You don't have to fill the silence when you're beside someone.

You don't have to explain why you're quiet.

You don't have to manage their response.

Because something about the alignment makes room for just being.

And that's rare.

In a world that constantly asks us to *say something*, to *show something*, to *prove something*, it's an incredible relief to simply sit beside someone and feel no need to perform.

That kind of stillness is not absence.

It's presence in its most honest form.

Being side by side also means learning the art of pause.

Stopping to look at something.

Sitting down when one of you is tired.

Shifting your body slightly when the mood changes.

These little acts, often unnoticed, are actually powerful signs of attunement.

They say, "I'm paying attention."

"I'll slow down when you need to."

"I won't rush ahead without you."

These are the things that make closeness sustainable.

Not grand gestures.

But steady ones.

Not all closeness needs to be declared.

Some of it just needs to be lived.

You find it in the easy repetition of shared tasks.

Making dinner together without a plan.

Folding laundry side by side, barely talking but fully together.

Cleaning up after a gathering, your movements crossing and overlapping like a practiced dance.

These moments don't demand deep connection.

But they *create* it, gradually, quietly.

The kind of bond that isn't built through conversation alone, but through cooperation.

Through rhythm.

Through being in the same space, doing the same thing, for no other reason than that you want to be near each other.

Closeness shows up in small agreements.

I'll carry this, if you carry that.

I'll start the car, you get the directions.

I'll chop, you stir.

No contracts.

No titles.

Just an unspoken rhythm of "we."

That "we" builds slowly, often without realization.

Until one day you catch yourself thinking not "What do I need?" but "What do *we* need?"

And suddenly, the shape of your day includes them.

Not out of obligation.

But out of reflex.

Like breathing.

Like knowing they'll be beside you when it matters.

Walking through life beside someone means matching more than speed.

It means noticing when they're distracted.

When they've grown quiet in a way that isn't peaceful.

When their silence holds weight instead of rest.

You don't have to fix it.

You don't even have to name it.

You just shift your presence to meet them where they are.

Slower. Quieter. Closer.

Sometimes your body says, "I've noticed," before your mouth ever does.

And sometimes, that's more than enough.

Being side by side makes room for contrast, too.

One of you might talk more.

The other might take longer to open up.

One of you might initiate plans.

The other might show care in more quiet, steady ways.

But this difference isn't a gap.

It's a balance.

When nearness is built on respect, not performance, you learn to trust each other's pace.

You don't expect them to move at your speed.

You just keep pace with them when it matters.

Not because you have to.

But because you want to.

Because something in you says: I'd rather move with you than move alone.

There's a tenderness in shared stillness.

Lying on the couch while music plays.

Sitting on a porch watching the rain.

Laying next to each other, not touching, not talking, just breathing.

These moments don't "progress" the relationship.

They don't clarify feelings.

They don't solve anything.

But they do something just as important.

They allow peace to settle between you.

And in a world where most of us are taught to earn connection, to chase it, to constantly prove our worth, that kind of settled peace is a quiet revolution.

To be near someone and know you don't have to be *doing* anything to deserve it.

That you can just be.

And be welcome.

Side by side, you learn to read a new kind of language.

The tap of a foot.

The deepening of a breath.

The way someone shifts in their seat when they're about to speak, or when they decide not to.

You learn to respond not with advice, but with space.

With a glance that says "I'm here."

With a pause that says "You don't have to hurry."

With a presence that says "We're okay, even in this quiet."

It's an intimacy built not on answers, but on attention.

You realize how much love, of all kinds, is communicated this way.

Through someone waiting beside you at the doctor's office.

Through someone driving the long way home because they know you like the view.

Through someone making room on the couch, even if they don't say a word.

These are not grand gestures.

They're not headline-worthy.

But they build something lasting.

Because they say: I see you.

I'm here.

I'll stay with you in this.

Sometimes, walking side by side is a way of remembering that you don't have to carry it all alone.

You don't even have to name what's heavy.

Just the feeling of another person near you, matching your steps, staying close, not needing you to be okay in order to stay, that can be enough.

Enough to keep going.

Enough to breathe more easily.

Enough to feel like maybe, just maybe, you're not on your own.

You won't always be in sync.

Sometimes they'll pull ahead.

Sometimes you'll fall behind.

Sometimes one of you will be distracted, restless, unsure.

But that's the beauty of walking side by side.

You learn how to circle back.

How to slow down.

How to reach for each other again without shame or scolding.

It's not about being perfectly aligned.

It's about being willing to keep adjusting.

Because you've decided: this is someone worth walking with.

Even when it's not easy.

Even when the path shifts.

Especially then.

The more time you spend beside someone, the more you begin to notice the subtle dance of presence.

How one of you begins a task and the other joins in.

How you fall into routines not because you planned them, but because they just made sense.

How you drift into conversation not from necessity, but from the ease of already being near.

That's the kind of closeness that doesn't clamor to be seen.

It just *is*, like background music that suddenly becomes your favorite part of the room.

This kind of relationship isn't built by intensity.

It's built by return.

By how you keep showing up.

By how you keep making space.

By how you keep saying, through small gestures: I'm here. I still want to be.

And it's that repetition, that calm, consistent staying, that begins to wrap itself around your ordinary life.

So many people think love is built in the extremes.

The high highs. The dramatic confessions. The urgent passion.

But this?

This is something steadier.

Side by side becomes a way of life.

You learn to read mood not just from words, but from posture.

They slump a little when they're overwhelmed.

They hum when they're content.

They start cleaning when they're anxious, or go quiet when they don't want to ask for help.

These small signals become familiar.

Not as problems to solve, but as invitations to support.

You say, "I've got this one."

Or, "You don't have to explain."

Or, "Let's take a break."

And sometimes, you don't say anything at all.

You just sit a little closer.

Move a little slower.

Let your presence do the steadying.

Side by side teaches patience.

Not every day is light.

Not every interaction is smooth.

Sometimes they're short with you. Sometimes you're distracted. Sometimes everything feels slightly off.

But when you've built something real, you don't panic.

You don't start questioning the foundation just because the weather changed.

You know how to wait it out.

You know how to let the quiet moments pass.

You know how to circle back when the words are ready.

This is a deeper kind of connection.

One that trusts the pattern, even when a piece of it falters.

In the closeness of daily life, you start to develop a kind of shorthand.

You look at each other and know it's time to go.

You finish each other's sentences, or don't need them finished at all.

You can tell what kind of day it's been by the sound of their footsteps.

This isn't magic.

It's just time.

Time plus care plus repetition.

These are the invisible roots of closeness.

Not glamorous.

Not always noticeable.

But essential.

They're what hold you together when life gets messy.

There's a difference between standing with someone and standing beside them.

To stand with someone is to support them when they fall.

To stand beside them is to be there before they do.

To walk the road, not just show up when the journey gets hard.

To notice before you're needed.

To be near without being called.

That kind of presence isn't flashy.

It's not the stuff of grand stories.

But it's the foundation of every relationship that lasts.

Being beside someone doesn't mean you always understand them.

It means you choose to stay when you don't.

You might not get why they're upset.

You might not feel the same way.

You might not even know what they need.

But you're willing to stay long enough to learn.

You're willing to sit in the not-knowing without making them feel alone in it.

That's one of the deepest kinds of love:

The willingness to remain, not just when things make sense, but when they don't.

This kind of nearness changes the way you move through the world.

You begin to think in plural.

"What do *we* want for dinner?"

"Will *they* be comfortable there?"

"Do *we* have time this weekend?"

You don't lose yourself, you expand.

You grow your awareness to include someone else, not as a burden, but as a presence you want to carry forward.

Side by side becomes not just a posture, but a mindset.

One that reshapes your sense of time, of space, of care.

Sometimes you'll walk together and talk the whole way.

Other times, you'll be silent for long stretches.

Neither means more than the other.

Both are valid.

Both are meaningful.

Because being beside someone means letting the moment be what it is, not what you think it should be.

You release the need to perform.

You step out of the pressure to make things perfect.

You simply share the path, and that is enough.

That kind of simplicity is rare.

And when you find it, you protect it.

Some of the most important moments in a relationship don't feel important when they happen.

They're the ones where you hand each other a cup of coffee without asking.

Where you sit on the same side of the room, just because it feels better that way.

Where one of you waits outside while the other runs inside the store, and you don't need to explain why, it's just how things go now.

These aren't highlights.

They're the in-between moments.

The glue.

But in time, you look back and realize: that's where the closeness lived.

Not in the milestones, but in the motions.

This is the gift of physical and emotional alignment:

You don't always have to think so hard.

You don't have to prepare the perfect thing to say.

You don't have to plan every step ahead.

You just keep showing up.

Side by side.

Again and again.

And what starts as effort slowly becomes rhythm.

Then routine.

Then something deeper, a kind of trust that lives in the body.

You stop asking, "Are we okay?" after every off day.

Because you *know* you're okay.

You've walked through enough together to trust the pattern.

Side-by-side closeness teaches you to value peace.

Not the absence of conflict, but the presence of calm.

You begin to notice how rare it is to be around someone who doesn't exhaust you.

Who doesn't need your attention all the time, but values it when it's given.

Who lets you be quiet, and doesn't take it personally.

This kind of peace isn't boring, it's healing.

It gives your nervous system room to settle.

CHAPTER 4: SIDE BY SIDE

It gives your heart a break from striving.

It allows your mind to rest inside connection instead of chasing it.

And once you've felt that kind of peace, you stop mistaking chaos for love.

In the company of someone who knows how to walk beside you, you begin to understand yourself more clearly.

Because you're no longer performing.

You're just present.

And presence reveals truth, not all at once, but gradually.

You learn what you reach for when you're tired.

What habits you fall into.

What kind of space you take up when no one's asking you to be smaller or louder or different.

And if the person beside you sees that, all of that, and stays?

You begin to feel safe not only with them, but with yourself.

That's one of the greatest gifts we give each other:

The space to be, without needing to adjust for someone else's comfort.

There's a unique comfort in physical closeness that doesn't demand touch.

When you sit next to each other and lean, but don't cling.

When your legs rest against each other casually.

When your steps align just because they do.

This isn't about possession or attraction.

It's about ease.

About knowing that nearness can be soft.

That physical presence doesn't always have to escalate.

That comfort itself can be a form of affection.

We often overlook this kind of touch, the kind that says,

"I'm not trying to take anything from you. I just want to be near."

And sometimes, that's the touch that matters most.

Shared presence builds shared memory.

Not just of events, but of feeling.

You'll remember the day you walked nowhere in particular, just to be together.

You'll remember the time you sat through a storm, saying almost nothing, and it became one of your favorite afternoons.

You'll remember that time the coffee shop was too loud, so you left and just wandered, and somehow, that felt like the best choice all day.

These are not milestones.

They're map points.

Moments you return to, emotionally, because they remind you what closeness really feels like.

Not dazzling.

But steady.

Not loud.

But lasting.

Being side by side is also an act of patience.

Because not every day will feel connected.

Not every hour will hold warmth.

Some days you'll be preoccupied, or grumpy, or simply off.

But even on those days, you stay near.

You share the space.

You wait for the warmth to return.

You don't run at the first sign of friction.

That kind of patience isn't passive.

It's powerful.

It says, "You don't have to be perfect for me to stay."

And when someone says that, with their body, with their time, with their calm, you learn to breathe a little easier.

You also learn that companionship doesn't erase solitude.

You can be side by side and still be in your own world.

Still reading your own book.

Still thinking your own thoughts.

The beauty of this kind of closeness is that it doesn't consume.

It coexists.

You don't have to collapse into each other to be connected.

You don't have to lose yourself to feel held.

You can just be, full and whole and present, next to someone doing the same.

And in that shared solitude, something quiet and rare emerges:

Two people, fully themselves, who choose to remain near.

Eventually, the idea of being side by side with someone becomes less about presence and more about partnership.

You're not just sharing a moment.

You're shaping a life.

You start to rely on each other in subtle ways.

One reaches for the keys, the other locks the door.

One starts the sentence, the other finishes it.

One stumbles, the other slows down without needing to ask why.

This is not dependency.

This is collaboration.

A quiet understanding that you each carry part of the rhythm now, not because you have to, but because you want to.

The longer you walk beside someone, the more clearly you understand the shape of your own steps.

You learn how you move when you're supported.

How you speak when you're not being rushed.

How your body relaxes when it knows someone is paying attention without trying to control.

And you learn what it means to offer that same steadiness in return.

This is the slow, steady trust that grows not from declarations, but from repetition.

From showing up when it would be easier not to.

From keeping pace even when life speeds up or stretches thin.

Sometimes you look back and realize how far you've come, not in distance, but in alignment.

Where once you walked nervously, now you move easily.

Where once you spoke with caution, now your voice flows freely.

Where once you tried to match pace, now you just... do.

It doesn't happen all at once.

It's not dramatic.

It's gradual, like the way two trees grow toward the same patch of sunlight, their branches bending toward each other over time.

You don't notice every inch of movement, but one day, you look up and you're surrounded by something that feels like home.

Closeness like this isn't the kind you write about in headlines.

It's not explosive or cinematic.

It doesn't demand attention.

It offers something quieter:

Reliability.

Tenderness.

Ease.

And in a world so loud, that kind of ease is a rare and radical thing.

The kind of love, in any form, that says,

"You don't have to dazzle me. Just be near."

"I won't ask you to carry everything, but I'll carry what I can."

"You don't have to perform. I just like the sound of your footsteps beside mine."

Of course, there are days when it's hard.

When the road feels long and your energy doesn't match.

When you want to be alone.

When they don't understand what you're going through.

But those days don't erase the closeness.

They clarify it.

Because side by side doesn't mean frictionless.

It means committed to returning.

To staying in step, even when the path twists.

To trusting the connection more than the discomfort of the moment.

You may not always feel aligned, but you know how to find your way back.

That's the difference between temporary company and true companionship.

Side by side means you start planning for each other without realizing it.

You grab an extra snack.

You choose the show you know they'll like.

You leave the light on when they're out late.

These aren't grand declarations.

They're built-in consideration.

They're the quiet way we say, "I'm thinking of you, even when you're not here."

And over time, those small acts add up.

They build the feeling of being held, not in arms, but in awareness.

To be carried in someone's daily thoughts is a kind of closeness that transcends distance.

You realize you don't need constant conversation to feel connected.

Sometimes the most meaningful part of the day is simply being in the same room.

They're reading. You're working.

You don't interrupt each other. You don't even speak.

But there's something deeply comforting in the shared stillness.

A reminder that love doesn't always have to be loud.

That attention doesn't always have to arrive as action.

That sometimes, the most intimate thing is to live your own life, quietly, fully, beside someone doing the same.

And sometimes, being side by side means walking through things you never expected.

Grief.

Change.

Distance.

The ache of uncertainty.

In those seasons, the pace might slow.

The silence might grow.

The path might feel unfamiliar.

But even then, nearness matters.

Even when there's nothing to fix.

Even when the answers don't come.

Even when all you can do is sit close and say, "I'm not leaving."

That, more than anything, is what side by side really means.

It means you stay.

Not just in joy, but in confusion.

Not just when it's easy, but when it's real.

So much of our lives are spent chasing connection.

Trying to impress. To captivate. To earn presence.

But true closeness, the kind that sits beside you quietly, day after day, isn't about earning.

It's about choosing.

Choosing to show up.

Choosing to adjust your pace.

Choosing to sit next to someone, even when you don't know what to say.

Choosing, again and again, to stay beside them, not because you have to, but because you still want to.

And that choice?

That's where real connection lives.

Chapter 5: The First Touch

Touch is the most ancient language.

Long before we had words, we reached.

To comfort, to connect, to say: I'm here. I see you. You're not alone.

And even now, with all we know how to say, sometimes the body still speaks more clearly.

A hand on a shoulder.

A hug held one second longer than usual.

Fingers brushing, on purpose or by accident, and everything suddenly feels realer than it did a moment ago.

Touch doesn't just confirm presence.

It *changes* it.

There's a moment before the first touch where everything is suspended.

You've been near each other, sitting close, walking in sync, sharing space.

There's trust. Comfort. Ease.

But now the distance is about to collapse completely.

And in that split second, right before skin meets skin, time slows.

You don't think in words anymore.

You feel.

The awareness sharpens.

The silence thickens.

And then, contact.

It might be the lightest thing.

A hand resting against yours.

A shoulder leaning in.

Fingers passing something back, and holding on just slightly longer than needed.

But it changes everything.

Because it's no longer hypothetical.

No longer imagined.

It's felt.

The spark becomes tangible.

The closeness becomes undeniable.

And no matter how small, that first touch is a threshold.

A movement from wondering to knowing.

Touch is not just physical. It's emotional.

It carries tone.

It carries meaning.

It carries risk.

To reach out is to say: I'm letting you closer. I'm letting you affect me. I'm allowing myself to be felt, and to feel.

Even the simplest contact can hold volumes.

A steady hand can say, "You're safe."

A trembling one might say, "I'm afraid, but I'm still here."

A casual brush might say, "I'm curious. Are you?"

We don't always know how to interpret these things.

But we feel them.

The body knows before the mind can explain.

The first time someone touches you with care, not out of duty, but desire, it's unforgettable.

Because it tells a different kind of truth.

One that words can't reach.

It's not about passion. Not yet.

It's about presence.

About the act of letting someone into your physical world, the space you guard most closely.

And when that space is met with tenderness?

With respect?

With a kind of unspoken reverence?

It stays with you.

There's a reason the first touch is often cautious.

Even if you've known each other for a while.

Even if the emotional intimacy has deepened.

Touch feels like a different kind of commitment.

It can't be undone in the same way a word can.

It lingers.

It imprints.

So we approach it carefully, not out of fear, but out of honor.

We reach slowly.

We wait for a return.

We listen, not just for permission, but for presence.

Because the point of touch isn't to take.

It's to share.

And that kind of sharing takes courage.

Sometimes the first touch doesn't happen in a moment of joy, but in a moment of pain.

You see someone struggling, and without thinking, you reach out.

Not to fix. Not to ask.

Just to say, "I'm with you in this."

A hand on their back.

A palm over theirs.

An arm around shoulders, no words spoken.

These moments might not be romantic.

But they are intimate.

Because they bridge the gap between separate experiences.

Because they say, "Your pain matters to me."

That is its own kind of closeness.

Consent, of course, is part of this.

Not just in the legal sense, in the emotional one.

To reach out without permission is to assume.

To reach out with awareness is to ask, even without words.

You notice body language.

You offer space before you cross it.

You let the other person decide if they want to meet you there.

This is not hesitation.

This is care.

Because true closeness isn't about claiming.

It's about being welcomed in.

And nothing builds trust like touch that listens.

Sometimes touch says what you can't.

When words get stuck.

When emotions run too high.

When silence feels too thick to cut through.

A hand can speak.

An embrace can say, "I'm sorry," or "I'm here," or "Don't leave."

A gentle squeeze can be a lifeline.

A steady presence can calm the chaos inside.

We spend so much time trying to find the right thing to say.

But sometimes, the right thing is already in your reach.

Literally.

The first touch is never just about contact.

It's about *choice*.

You choose to reach.

You choose to allow.

And if it's done with presence, with care, with full awareness of its meaning, it becomes more than a moment.

It becomes memory.

The kind that stays in the skin.

The kind that replays in quiet hours.

The kind you return to not because of what happened, but because of how it felt.

Real. Grounding. Alive.

And from that first point of contact, something begins.

Touch, when mutual and mindful, becomes an echo, something you feel long after the moment ends.

A hand resting on your arm.

The press of a shoulder against yours.

A warm palm on your back as you step into an unfamiliar space.

Even after the contact fades, its impression remains.

The body remembers what kindness felt like.

And that memory softens you.

It reminds you that connection isn't only in what's said.

It lives in the warmth that lingered.

The comfort that settled.

The moment you knew, without explanation: *they meant that.*

As physical closeness grows, so does its language.

You begin to understand the difference between gesture and intimacy.

Between the way someone taps your shoulder to get your attention, and the way they rest their hand there when they want you to stay.

Between a casual high five and fingers laced together under the table.

These moments aren't about grand romance, they're about attunement.

Each touch carries tone.

Each one says, "I know you'll feel this," and "I hope it lands well."

That level of care, of intention, is what turns contact into communication.

There are times when you want to reach out but hesitate.

Not because you're unsure of your own desire, but because you're honoring theirs.

You don't want to cross a threshold they haven't opened.

And that awareness, in itself, is an act of love.

Because restraint is sometimes more intimate than action.

Choosing *not* to touch when the other person isn't ready, or when the moment isn't right, shows that their comfort matters more than your impulse.

That's the foundation of safety.

That's how you earn deeper trust.

By showing that what you feel will never override what they need.

Eventually, you begin to recognize which kinds of touch offer support, and which offer connection.

The hand on someone's back when they cry? That's grounding.

The hug after a long day? That's shared relief.

The small squeeze of a hand during a difficult moment? That's reassurance.

None of these gestures are complex.

But they are intentional.

They say:

"I see you."

"I feel this too."

"I'm here, and I won't leave when things get hard."

They don't try to solve anything.

They just join you in the moment.

And that kind of joining is what makes touch so powerful.

Sometimes the smallest touch creates the biggest shift.

Not because of what it means in the moment, but because of what it unlocks going forward.

A hand held in silence opens the door for a conversation that couldn't have happened otherwise.

A forehead resting against another's breaks the tension between two people who didn't know how to say "I forgive you."

A pinky finger finding another in a crowded room says, "I found you. I didn't forget."

Touch isn't always about escalation.

It's often about recognition.

The act of saying, "I see you still. Even now. Especially now."

In some relationships, physical contact becomes a rhythm.

A form of checking in.

A hand on the lower back when passing in the kitchen.

A knee bump under the table.

A hand resting briefly in another's lap on a long drive.

These aren't interruptions.

They're threads.

A way of staying connected, even when the conversation stops.

A way of saying, without words, "You still matter to me, even in the middle of this ordinary day."

That kind of touch is not loud.

But it's consistent.

And consistency is what builds emotional security.

There's also the question of timing.

Not all touch is received equally at every moment.

What feels comforting on one day might feel overwhelming the next.

What used to mean one thing might shift in meaning as the relationship evolves.

Touch, like language, requires translation.

It changes.

It deepens.

It adapts.

You learn to ask, even without words.

To feel the mood.

To wait for reciprocity.

And when that yes comes, the leaning in, the softening, the hand that reaches back, it feels all the more profound.

Because it was chosen.

Not assumed.

Not taken.

Given.

Physical closeness can also bring clarity.

Sometimes the first touch confirms what you already knew, that there's something here.

Other times, it surprises you.

You thought you were ready, but something about the contact feels off.

Too soon. Too much. Too vulnerable.

That's okay too.

Because touch isn't a contract.

It's a moment.

And moments are allowed to shift.

You're allowed to step back.

You're allowed to learn through the trying.

That's how you grow into yourself, and into others, without losing your footing.

But when it *does* feel right?

When the first touch lands gently, clearly, fully?

It becomes a new beginning.

A chapter opened not with words, but with weight.

With warmth.

With a shared breath that says, "This is something now."

As touch becomes more familiar, it begins to say things words can't keep up with.

Where once you hesitated, now you reach.

Not constantly. Not automatically.

But confidently. Deliberately.

You've felt the difference, between contact that reassures and contact that claims, between being held and being gripped, between being touched because someone cares and being touched because someone *wants*.

And that difference shapes how you offer yourself in return.

Touch, when it's safe, becomes a kind of permission.

To soften.

To settle.

To let your guard down without losing yourself.

Not every touch needs to mean something dramatic.

Some are just gentle reminders:

"I'm still here."

"You're not alone."

"I like being near you."

These small gestures, the thumb rubbed against a hand, the arm that brushes yours in passing, the playful nudge that invites laughter, they aren't loud.

But they're lasting.

Because they build a kind of dialogue.

A silent, continuous "yes" to each other's presence.

There's an intimacy in physical comfort that doesn't require closeness to be intense.

Falling asleep beside someone.

Reaching across a couch to rest your hand where theirs already is.

Sharing warmth under a blanket in a room gone quiet.

You're not moving toward something.

You're just being in it.

The moment isn't about leading anywhere.

It's about staying.

Staying near.

Staying open.

Staying soft.

And sometimes, that's the bravest thing two people can do,

Choose to stay, even when they could be elsewhere.

Even when nothing is being said.

Touch is a mirror, too.

It reflects how you feel, not just about them, but about yourself in their presence.

You reach more easily when you feel safe.

You hold back when something inside still aches.

You notice how you flinch, or freeze, or relax depending on how they touch you.

You notice how your own gestures change when trust deepens.

Sometimes, the way someone's hand rests on your back reminds you that you've never had that kind of gentleness before.

And the realization feels like warmth and grief all at once.

Touch can heal.

But first, it often reveals.

There are moments when touch is all you have.

A hospital room.

A hard goodbye.

A breakdown you didn't see coming.

In those moments, there are no perfect words.

There's only presence.

A hand that holds yours when nothing can be fixed.

A body that stays close when the rest of the world pulls away.

A forehead pressed to yours to say, "I'm with you, even in this."

And sometimes, that kind of touch does more than language ever could.

It says, "We're in this together."

And that's enough.

As comfort deepens, touch becomes both quieter and more meaningful.

You no longer think about every gesture.

But you also don't take them for granted.

You recognize the weight of a head resting on your shoulder.

The way someone lets themselves lean into your side during a movie.

The silent understanding of a hand finding yours in a crowded room.

These moments don't demand attention.

They don't need explanation.

But they shape the way you remember the day.

They become anchors,

proof that closeness was not just felt, but embodied.

Sometimes touch helps you return to yourself.

After a long day.

After a difficult conversation.

After feeling scattered, lost, or overwhelmed.

A steady hand on your back grounds you.

Fingers gently threading through yours slows your breathing.

The quiet embrace that asks nothing reminds you that you don't have to hold it all alone.

This is one of the great gifts of physical presence:

It offers a home for your nervous system.

It lets your body believe what your mind may still doubt, that you're safe, that you're wanted, that you're not carrying this by yourself.

But none of this works without trust.

Touch without trust is tension.

It makes the skin brace, not soften.

It makes presence feel like pressure, not care.

That's why the most meaningful gestures aren't the boldest, they're the most considered.

The pause before a hand is placed.

The awareness in a hug that doesn't linger too long.

The ability to stop, instantly, when something shifts.

Real closeness isn't just about offering yourself.

It's about noticing when the other person needs space more than they need you.

That noticing?

That's what turns affection into love.

With time, the body begins to remember who feels safe.

It leans into certain people instinctively.

It knows which kinds of contact feel calming.

It recognizes the difference between being wanted and being welcomed.

And when you find someone whose touch always brings you back to yourself,

someone whose hand never feels like a demand but like a presence,

you hold onto that.

Because it's rare.

And it's real.

And it reminds you what it means to be held *without being handled*.

And from that moment on, every new contact carries a bit of that memory.

That threshold crossed.

That space once held by silence now filled with presence.

The distance is gone.

And something real has arrived.

Sometimes, the first meaningful touch doesn't come with music or moonlight or anything resembling a movie moment.

It happens in the middle of a conversation, or a moment of worry, or even just a laugh.

One of you reaches without thinking, and the other doesn't pull away.

And there it is.

The spark. The shift.

The instant where physical nearness catches up with emotional connection.

It doesn't announce itself.

It doesn't ask for attention.

But something opens.

And neither of you forget it.

What makes the first touch so powerful isn't the act itself.

It's the permission.

It says:

"You can come closer now."

"I trust you in this space."

"I want you to feel this, too."

That permission is what softens the moment.

It's what makes it tender instead of tense.

Inviting instead of overwhelming.

And when that permission is mutual, when both people lean, even a little, it creates a new kind of closeness.

A new kind of knowing.

There are touches that take your breath away.

Not because they're bold, but because they're *honest*.

The moment someone's hand grazes yours and you feel every nerve wake up.

The way their arm rests around your shoulder and your body instinctively exhales.

The brush of fingers down your back that says more than a dozen conversations ever could.

Honest touch doesn't perform.

It doesn't try to convince.

It just reveals.

It says: *This is how I feel.*

This is what I mean.

This is me, right here, reaching for you.
And in return, your body speaks back.
It leans in.
It allows.
It says: *I feel it, too.*
That's how a shared rhythm begins.
One where neither person has to lead, because both are listening.
To breath. To shift. To silence. To each other.
Touch becomes a dance.
Unchoreographed, but meaningful.
Spontaneous, but attuned.
You don't have to talk about it to know you've found the rhythm.
You just feel it, in the way they don't flinch when you reach.
In the way you no longer hesitate to rest your head against their chest.
In the way presence becomes contact, and contact becomes comfort.
Touch can also be a way of remembering.
Of returning to something you've both known.
The hand held during a hospital visit.
The hug after a long absence.
The squeeze before one of you leaves for a while.
These are the touches that anchor you, not in fantasy, but in real life.
They remind you: *we've been here before.*
We've made it through.
We'll make it again.
Touch doesn't just mark beginnings.
It marks endurance.
The ongoing choice to reach for each other, even when it would be easier not to.
There are nights when a hand on your back will mean more than any grand speech.
There are days when someone brushing the hair from your face will feel like the kindest thing they've ever done.
These gestures are small, but they echo.

Because what they really say is:

"I notice you."

"I want to help carry this."

"You are not invisible."

And in a world that moves so quickly, that asks us to be so much, so often, there is nothing more healing than to be gently, lovingly, *noticed.*

As touch becomes more natural, it starts to fill the spaces where words might not fit.

You don't always need to say, "I missed you."

You can show up, wrap your arms around them, and just stay.

You don't have to explain, "I'm hurting."

You can let your hand rest in theirs, and they'll know.

Touch becomes a kind of language.

And the fluency deepens with time.

You know what kind of touch calms them.

They know how to hold you when you can't speak.

This isn't about physical need.

It's about emotional fluency.

The quiet, steady knowledge of how to be present without having to be perfect.

Even when things are hard, touch can soften the edge.

After an argument, it might be the first hand that reaches, not to fix, but to reconnect.

Not to erase, but to say, "I still want to find you again."

And that's the truth of any meaningful relationship:

You won't always agree.

You won't always understand.

But you can still choose to reach.

Not for resolution.

But for remembrance.

To say, "We're still here."

"We're still us."

Of course, there are times when touch needs space.

When emotions run too high.

When one or both of you feel raw or uncertain.

When what you need isn't contact, but quiet.

And that, too, is part of the language.

Learning to step back.

Learning to honor pause.

Learning to trust that connection isn't measured by how often you reach out, but by how thoughtfully you do.

This, more than anything, is what makes touch meaningful:

It's not how often it happens.

It's how *present* you are when it does.

The most powerful touches often go unnoticed by the world.

They're not the ones shared in public.

They're not posted or praised.

They happen in quiet corners, where presence is enough, and performance has no place.

They're the ones you remember not because of how they looked, but because of how they felt.

A hand reaching for yours without fanfare.

Fingers brushing your cheek before sleep.

An arm around your waist in the kitchen while the coffee brews.

Small, ordinary, profound.

Because the first touch may begin everything,

but the continued touch is what builds something lasting.

Over time, you start to see how touch shapes trust.

You notice how your body responds to theirs.

How the space between you feels softer, safer.

How simply standing near them steadies you.

They don't have to hold you to be holding you.

Sometimes their nearness is enough.

Sometimes it's the look before the touch, the silent "may I?" that's already understood, that tells you they care.

This is how trust moves into the body.

Slowly.

Quietly.

Fully.

And once it's there, everything begins to rest.

The more you offer each other presence, the more the body believes: *this is safe.*

This is wanted.

This is okay.

And with that belief, you begin to open.

Not just physically, emotionally.

You laugh more easily.

You cry more freely.

You speak without rehearsing every word in your head.

Because you're no longer just being seen.

You're being held.

And that kind of safety is not loud.

It's not dramatic.

But it's deeply transformational.

It allows love, in any form, to grow roots.

Touch won't fix everything.

But it doesn't need to.

It's not about repair, it's about reminder.

It says, "I'm still here."

It says, "You matter."

It says, "Even in this mess, I won't let go."

And sometimes, that's all we need to carry on.

Not solutions.

Not certainty.

Just someone beside us, hand in hand, shoulder to shoulder, choosing to stay.

That choice, repeated over time, becomes something real and rare.

Not because it's perfect.

But because it's real.

You'll remember the first touch.

Not just where it happened, but how your body reacted.

How the air felt.

How everything slowed down for just a second before it happened.

You'll remember the look in their eyes.

The space that was crossed.

The internal yes you didn't say out loud but meant with everything you had.

And you'll remember what followed.

How the tone changed.

How the space softened.

How closeness became a little less hypothetical, and a little more lived.

The first touch is a threshold.

But it's not the destination.

It's an opening.

An offering.

A question.

Do you feel this too?

Can we move from here, together?

If the answer is yes, something begins.

If the answer is no, something is still learned.

Because even reaching without return teaches you about yourself, your courage, your desire, your honesty.

Touch is never meaningless when it's chosen with care.

Even when it's not returned the way you hope.

Eventually, the novelty fades, and what remains is intention.

You still reach, but you don't need to hesitate.

You still hold, but not to convince.

You touch to affirm.

To steady.

To show up.

And if you're lucky, so do they.

You find each other in gestures that are no longer milestones, but maintenance.

Not beginnings, but continuity.

This is how touch becomes love.

Not the kind you fall into, the kind you *build*.

The body remembers safety.

And the first person who teaches you what it means to be held gently, kindly, without pressure, they stay with you.

Even if the relationship changes.

Even if time moves on.

You carry the memory in your muscles.

The imprint of being cared for not just emotionally, but physically, with kindness, with awareness, with respect.

And because of that, you move forward differently.

You offer your own touch more gently.

You understand what it means to hold without taking.

To reach without rushing.

You become someone else's first safe touch, and that's a gift that never ends with you.

Chapter 6: Entangled

There comes a point in closeness when lines begin to blur.

Where does your story end and theirs begin?

Where is the boundary between comfort and connection, between holding and being held?

It doesn't happen all at once.

It happens slowly, like threads weaving together over time.

A shared night. A long look. A quiet morning where neither of you rushes to leave.

You wake up beside someone and realize you didn't just sleep next to them, you *shared rest*.

You breathed in rhythm.

You found stillness *together*.

This is intimacy. Not performance. Not promise. Just presence, deepened.

Intimacy isn't always loud.

Sometimes it's the softest thing,

The way your knee brushes theirs under a table.

The way your hand finds theirs in the dark, not because it needs to, but because it *wants* to.

The way you both forget what you were talking about because you got distracted by the moment itself.

In these moments, bodies stop being strangers.

They begin to memorize each other.

Not in a rushed or dramatic way, but like learning the shape of your own breath.

Familiar.

Reassuring.

Steady.

As the physical becomes more natural, so does the emotional.

You speak with more depth.

You listen with less fear.

You let silence hang longer, because you trust it now.

It's no longer about *impressing* each other.

It's about *inviting* each other further in.

Your stories aren't curated anymore.

They're shared freely.

You laugh at your own awkwardness.

You talk about your fears in a way you never used to.

And what's wild is, they stay.

Not because they're obligated.

Because they *want to*.

This is where entanglement begins.

Not in control.

Not in ownership.

But in mutual presence, offered, received, returned.

You feel their emotions in your body now.

When they're quiet, something in you leans in.

When they're anxious, your chest tightens too.

You don't carry it for them, but you feel it with them.

That's the difference between being involved and being *entwined*.

You haven't lost yourself.

You've opened yourself.

And in that openness, you've become part of something larger than just your own life.

There's a unique closeness that comes with physical intimacy that's not just about attraction, it's about trust.

Lying in bed together, half-asleep, knowing you don't have to fill the space with anything.

Their breath becomes familiar.

Their weight beside you becomes comforting.

You adjust your body to theirs without thinking.

It's not about desire, though that may be present.

It's about comfort.

Safety.

The joy of just being *near*, skin to skin, without urgency.

This is not about what might happen.

It's about what already *is*.

In these moments, time stretches.

An hour feels like a chapter.

A single morning feels like its own lifetime.

You move slowly because there's no reason to rush.

You speak softly because volume feels unnecessary.

You linger, not to prolong anything, but because you genuinely want to be there.

That's what entanglement does.

It makes you want to *stay*.

Not because you have to.

Not because there's nowhere else to go.

But because this space, this closeness, has become a kind of home.

But even in intimacy, there's a need for balance.

Entanglement isn't about merging completely.

It's about being near without dissolving.

You learn what it means to be yourself *with* someone, not *inside* them.

You keep your thoughts, even as you share them.

You keep your voice, even as you harmonize.

That balance is delicate.

And it takes care to maintain.

But when both people hold it well, the result is something rare:

A connection where no one disappears, and yet everyone feels held.

Sometimes you find yourself missing them while they're right beside you, not because they're distant, but because the moment is so tender you already feel it ending.

That's the strange beauty of intimacy:

It heightens everything.

The laughter feels louder.

The pauses feel longer.

The touch feels etched into you, like a memory forming in real time.

And sometimes, without meaning to, you start grieving its eventual passing, even while you're still inside it.

That's how precious it is.

That's how deeply you've been moved.

Entanglement doesn't mean constant closeness.

It means intentional closeness.

A glance that says more than a sentence.

A shared breath that calms both of you.

A night spent saying nothing at all, and knowing it was enough.

It's not about drama.

It's about depth.

It's not about intensity.

It's about presence.

And once you've felt that kind of presence, once you've *given* it and been *received* in it, it's hard to go back to anything less.

There's a moment in closeness where your thoughts begin to tangle with theirs.

Not because you've lost your own mind, but because your worlds are no longer separate.

You start to think of them in small decisions:

Would they like this song?

Should I wait and tell them this in person?

I wonder what they'd say about this.

You check in, not out of obligation, but instinct.

You want them to know where you are, what you're feeling, how your day's been, not to report, but to *include*.

This is the slow weaving of lives.

Not all at once.

But thread by thread.

Entanglement doesn't erase individuality.

It honors it.

You remain fully yourself, with your own thoughts, your own pace, your own breath, and yet, they're there.

Inside your day.

Inside your choices.

Inside the quiet moments when you feel their presence without needing them to speak.

This is not possession.

This is companionship, grown close.

And the closeness no longer feels like something you're building.

It just *is*.

Like a rhythm you return to.

Like a center you carry.

Physical intimacy deepens too, not just in action, but in awareness.

You notice how they breathe when they're falling asleep.

You know how to adjust your body to let theirs rest easier.

You hold them without thinking, not for comfort, but for grounding, yours and theirs.

Touch becomes natural.

Not constant, not demanded.

Just available.

Always available.

A hand brushing a shoulder in the kitchen.

A foot finding another under the blanket.

A head resting lightly on a chest, just for a moment, just because.

This is not routine.

This is ritual.

Shared. Repeated. Chosen.

In this kind of closeness, the body becomes a language.

You learn what different kinds of silence mean.

You learn which touches say, "I need space," and which say, "I need you closer."

You learn that intimacy doesn't always look like passion.

Sometimes it looks like forehead to forehead in the dark, neither of you speaking, both of you breathing a little slower.

Sometimes it looks like holding hands after a long day without needing to talk about it.

Sometimes it looks like falling asleep with your backs touching, not because you're distant, but because you trust the space between you.

That trust is everything.

There's a kind of freedom in closeness when it's chosen, not clung to.

You don't hold on out of fear.

You don't rush to close every gap.

You let space stretch when it needs to, knowing you can come back to each other without anxiety.

This is what entangled love, in any form, learns over time:

Proximity without pressure.

Connection without clutching.

Intimacy without intrusion.

You're not constantly inside each other's lives.

But you're always inside each other's awareness.

And that, in itself, is enough.

There's a comfort that grows in bodies that have learned to rest together.

You recognize how they shift when they're waking up.

You know the sound of their sleep.

You trace the patterns of nearness like landmarks in a familiar place.

This is when the body says, *we're safe here.*

It doesn't startle when they reach for you.

It doesn't flinch when they touch the parts you once hid.

It relaxes.

Because trust has moved beyond the surface.

Because affection has become part of the architecture of your togetherness.

You start to realize that intimacy isn't always about what's added.

Sometimes it's about what falls away.

The need to explain.

The need to impress.

The armor you didn't know you were still wearing.

In true closeness, these things get softer.

You stop performing.

You stop protecting.

And slowly, you become more *yourself*, because someone is there who welcomes the truth of who you are, even when it's quiet, even when it's messy.

That's what entanglement does when it's healthy.

It doesn't consume you.

It *reveals* you.

But even the deepest closeness has its edges.

You'll hit places where your needs don't match.

Where one of you wants more and the other wants stillness.

Where one of you needs closeness and the other needs space.

And here's the truth: this doesn't mean you're breaking.

It means you're human.

It means the connection is real.

Because only real closeness *asks* us to grow.

It shows us where our habits meet someone else's heart.

Where our fears meet someone else's tenderness.

And when both people are willing to stay, not to control, but to understand, intimacy expands.

There's a kind of quiet joy that comes from this stage of connection.

It doesn't always sparkle.

It doesn't always stir butterflies.

But it brings you home.

You cook together without talking much.

You fold blankets and brush teeth and feed pets and pay bills, and somehow, even in the ordinariness, everything feels full.

Because you're not alone.

Because you're known.

And even in the parts that don't feel cinematic, you find something beautiful.

Not because of what's happening.

But because of *who* it's happening with.

The more time you spend entangled with someone, the more your inner world changes shape.

Not to match theirs, but to make room for them.

You begin to notice how they influence the way you see things.

The way you slow down in moments you used to rush.

The way your patience stretches, not because you've become someone else, but because something in you wants to stay connected.

This is the reshaping of the heart.

Not under pressure.

But through presence.

You've started living in response to each other.

Not reaction, *response.*

Thoughtful. Conscious. Mutual.

This is when you start to feel the "we" even in your solitude.

You walk through your day and they're with you, not physically, but emotionally.

Their voice echoes in your decisions.

Their preferences cross your mind at the grocery store.

Their reactions drift through your memory when something funny or hard or strange happens.

This isn't codependence.

This is emotional continuity.

A shared inner thread that doesn't require contact to feel real.

Because connection, at this point, has outgrown the room.

It's woven into the way you move through the world.

In physical closeness, your bodies adjust naturally.

You know how they sleep, how to leave them space when they need it, how to pull them closer when they stir.

You learn to kiss with less performance and more presence.

To hold without expectation.

To be near without needing more than what the moment gives.

Intimacy becomes less about arrival and more about rhythm.

Less about what happens, and more about *how* it happens, slowly, attentively, without rush or pressure.

And you begin to recognize: this is what it means to *be with* someone.

Not just in location.

In *everything*.

Sometimes, being entangled means being quiet together for longer than usual, letting the moment breathe instead of trying to fill it.

It means trusting that silence doesn't mean distance.

That a lack of words doesn't mean a lack of care.

That nearness can deepen without narration.

You might sit beside each other reading, or stand in the kitchen cooking separately, or rest without talking, and still feel completely connected.

Because when intimacy is this strong, it doesn't need constant tending.

It just needs respect.

You don't have to prove the bond.

You simply return to it.

There's a kind of calm that arrives when someone has seen all your different selves, and stayed.

They've seen you tired.

Anxious.

Joyful.

Grieving.

They've seen you when you didn't know what you needed.

When you weren't easy to reach.

When you didn't even like yourself.

And still, they didn't step back.

They didn't flinch.

They didn't rush in to fix you either.

They just remained, available, attentive, honest.

And because of that, you trust them with more.

Not as reward.

As recognition.

Because they've proven their care doesn't depend on the version of you they get.

Entanglement brings its own quiet tensions too.

There will be moments when your closeness feels overwhelming, when you need to step back to find your own rhythm again.

Not because you love them less.

But because you remember who you are more clearly in solitude.

And this is part of the balance:

Learning to let yourself drift to your own center now and then, without fear of disconnection.

In healthy closeness, space isn't a threat.

It's part of the trust.

A pause that allows you to return even deeper.

A breath that strengthens the bond instead of loosening it.

You come to understand that love isn't always about intensity, it's about integration.

They're not your *everything*.

They're just *part of everything* now.

You don't lose your identity in them.

You expand it around them.

They become part of your rituals.

Your language.

Your landscape.

And you, too, become part of theirs, not as a demand, but as a rhythm they choose.

Over and over again.

You stop needing big gestures to feel cared for.

You see it in the small things:

The way they remember how you take your coffee.

The way they wait to press play until you're in the room.

The way they put your phone on the charger without a word.

These things aren't grand.

But they're specific.

And specificity is one of the deepest forms of love.

It says, "I know you."

"I pay attention."

"I've chosen you not in theory, but in practice."

Entanglement doesn't mean dependency.

It means mutual shaping.

They influence you, yes, but you influence them too.

The way they respond to you has softened.

The way they speak to you has grown kinder.

The way they move through their day now includes you, in little ways they never would've expected.

This is how shared lives form.

Not by merging.

By *mirroring*, gently, deliberately, without erasing either person.

It's a slow echo.

And it deepens over time.

Entanglement, at its best, doesn't trap you.

It expands you.

You don't lose your freedom.

You find it refined.

Because now, your choices carry more awareness.

Not pressure, presence.

You're not just considering your path.

You're holding someone else's steps in mind too.

Not to carry their weight.

But to walk with it.

To walk with *them*.

This is the difference between being alone and being together:

You still move forward.

But you don't move *only* for yourself.

And something about that changes how you hold everything, time, pain, joy, even yourself.

The body, too, becomes part of the story.

Not just in moments of intimacy, but in the ordinary ways you reach for each other without thinking.

The hand you place on their shoulder when passing by.

The leg you stretch across the bed to find them in the morning.

The hug you offer without a word, simply because the day asked too much of both of you.

These gestures don't carry expectation.

They carry recognition.

They say, "I see you."

They say, "I know how you feel before you say it."

They say, "We're in this."

And sometimes, they say all of that just by staying near.

There's a strange comfort in realizing how predictable someone has become to you, not in a boring way, but in the way familiarity allows for relaxation.

You know how they'll respond when you're stressed.

You know what food they'll want when they're tired.

You know the quiet ways they apologize.

You know the moments they retreat, not to hide, but to heal.

This knowing becomes a kind of emotional shorthand.

You don't have to ask.

You don't have to guess.

You simply *sense*.

That sensing is the fruit of time.

And of care.

And of shared attention.

You also become aware of the weight of your own presence.

How your tone affects their body.

How your silence shapes the room.

How the way you walk into a space either invites ease or tension.

This awareness isn't pressure, it's a privilege.

To know that your presence *matters* to someone.

That how you show up isn't just about you anymore.

It's part of a dynamic.

A shared field.

And once you know that, you begin to move with more intention.

Not to manage perception.

But to offer steadiness.

To offer care.

Sometimes entanglement feels like building a house together, one quiet moment at a time.

Each conversation, a brick.

Each night spent beside each other, a beam.

Each choice to stay gentle when it would've been easier to shut down, a window.

And over time, that structure becomes something you live inside.

Not perfectly.

Not without storms.

But strong.

Sturdy.

Yours.

You begin to trust the foundation more than the feeling of the day.

You know that a hard moment doesn't mean collapse.

Because this, *this*, was built carefully.

And it can hold.

Entanglement is not about fusion.

It's about *connection without confusion*.

You still know where you end and they begin.

You just choose to meet at the edges more often.

To sit together in the overlap.

To lean when you could stand alone, not because you can't hold yourself, but because you're allowed to rest sometimes.

You learn how to ask without apology.

How to give without depletion.

How to carry *with* instead of *for*.

That's maturity.

That's intimacy with integrity.

Even in conflict, you can feel the bond.

The way you both fight *for* the connection, not just from your corner.

The way you circle back, even after raised voices or tired miscommunications.

The way you say, "Let's not let this be the thing that separates us."

That's what makes entanglement durable.

Not the absence of difficulty, the presence of return.

The commitment to repair.

To understand.

To remember what brought you close in the first place, and why it's worth preserving.

Even on the days it feels complicated.

There are moments when your closeness will scare you.

Not because it's unsafe.

But because it's real.

Because suddenly you can see how much you've come to rely on their voice.

Their presence.

Their way of anchoring you when the world feels uncertain.

And you'll ask:

"What happens if they go?"

"What happens if I lose this?"

These questions don't mean weakness.

They mean *love*.

They mean you've allowed yourself to feel something that could hurt.

And still, *you chose to feel it anyway.*

That's not fragility.

That's courage.

Over time, the boundaries between physical and emotional closeness start to blur completely.

You hold each other in the kitchen and it feels like forgiveness.

You brush a hand across their cheek and it feels like understanding.

You sit in silence after a hard conversation and it feels like grace.

These aren't just touches.

They're gestures of care, embodied.

And you begin to realize:

The body remembers kindness.

The heart recognizes presence.

And love, in its most lasting form, is often expressed not in words, but in *the way we stay.*

At some point, you look up and realize you no longer think of the connection as new.

It's not a question anymore.

It's a presence.

You don't wonder if they'll stay, they're already here.

You don't calculate your steps, you're already walking in rhythm.

What once felt like something forming now feels like something formed.

Not perfect. Not finished. But *real.*

The kind of closeness you no longer need to hold tightly, because it holds *you.*

This is where the language of touch changes, too.

You don't have to read into every handhold.

You don't have to analyze every gesture.

The meaning is already known.

When they reach for you, it isn't about proving affection, it's about *being* affectionate.

When you press your forehead to theirs, it isn't to say anything specific, it's to say, "I'm here. You're here. That's enough."

Touch becomes less symbolic.

More integrated.

Less about reassurance.

More about rhythm.

You move with each other now, not toward each other.

And that shift, that comfort, is a sign of something lasting.

Emotional intimacy reaches this point, too.

You don't always need long talks to feel close.

You don't need daily validation to feel wanted.

You've built something sturdy enough to survive the quiet.

You trust each other's care.

You trust the pauses between conversations.

You trust that if something needs to be said, it will be.

And in that trust, your inner world settles.

Because intimacy isn't just what you share, it's what you *no longer feel the need to protect*.

This kind of closeness isn't passive.

It's active in quiet ways.

The way you keep showing up.

The way you notice what's unspoken.

The way you forgive, not because it's easy, but because you care more about connection than being right.

You stop keeping score.

You stop performing your needs.

You start saying things plainly.

"I need help."

"I'm afraid."

"I don't know."

And the beautiful thing? They stay.

Not out of obligation, out of *wanting to stay in the room with the truth*.

That's what makes entanglement beautiful.

When love becomes this steady, you might wonder where the excitement went.

But look again. It's still there.

It just shows up differently now.

In the way they look at you across the room.

In the surprise coffee on a hard day.

In the way their hand finds yours on instinct, not ceremony.
This is love as *lived-in*.
Not as fire, as warmth.
Not as pursuit, as partnership.
Not as spectacle, as shared life.
And shared life, while quieter, lasts longer.
You start to notice how closeness expands your capacity.
Not just to love, but to *live*.
You're more patient with others.
You forgive yourself more easily.
You speak more kindly.
You carry less fear.
Why?
Because you're no longer bracing alone.
You have somewhere to land.
You know what it's like to be received.
And once you've been received fully,
once someone has held your joy and your pain without flinching,
you become braver.
Not just in the relationship.
In the world.
Entanglement becomes a kind of compass.
It doesn't control your direction.
But it reminds you what matters as you move.
It shapes how you choose your words.
How you treat strangers.
How you care for yourself.
Because love, when it's real, when it's mutual, when it's steady,
it doesn't just touch the parts of you that feel lovable.
It reaches the places you never thought deserved attention.
And it tells them:
"You are worthy, too."
"You are not too much."

"You are not too alone."
And with that message internalized, you begin to live differently.
In the best moments, you don't even think about how close you are.
You just live.
You just wake up together and move through the morning.
You just rest near each other in silence.
You just walk into the room knowing it's better because they're in it.
And that unthinking nearness, that seamless comfort, is a gift.
Because closeness that doesn't require effort is rare.
Not because it's easy.
But because it's *earned*.
Through the early risks.
Through the slow trust.
Through the choice to stay, again and again, when it would've been easier to retreat.
Eventually, you stop measuring the relationship in milestones.
You stop needing markers of progress.
Because what you have is already rooted.
Already alive.
Already enough.
You no longer need a reason to be close.
You just are.
You no longer need the high points to feel love.
You feel it in the middle of the week.
In the dishes being done.
In the way they remember to leave the porch light on when you're coming home late.
That's the shift.
From touch as confirmation to touch as continuation.
From emotion as spark to emotion as presence.
Entanglement isn't the end of the story.
It's where the real story begins.
Where presence becomes pattern.

Where attention becomes care.

Where care becomes something you return to, even on the hardest days.

It doesn't mean you won't ever feel distant.

But it means you'll always know the way back.

Because now you carry the map together.

You've built something not just with feeling, but with choice.

Not just with intensity, but with intention.

And that kind of closeness?

It lasts.

Not because it's easy.

But because you both keep choosing to hold it.

Chapter 7: The Spaces We Keep

Closeness is beautiful, but it's not weightless.
Even the healthiest connection carries its own gravity.
The longer you stay near someone, the more their energy wraps around yours.

The more you care, the more sensitive you become to their presence, and their absence.

And the more entangled you get, the easier it is to forget where you end and they begin.

This is not a flaw.

This is the nature of intimacy.

But every bond, no matter how rooted, still needs room to breathe.

Space isn't a threat to closeness.

It's part of how closeness stays alive.

There comes a point where even the most fulfilling connection can feel heavy.

Not because anything is wrong.

But because you've been carrying each other too tightly, too constantly.

Because you haven't exhaled on your own in a while.

You start to feel it in small ways.

You delay responding to messages, even when you want to be present.

You hesitate to make plans.

You feel touched out, talked out, emotionally full.

And that fullness, when ignored, turns to fatigue.

You still love them.

You still want the relationship.

But your system is asking for space.

And that request deserves to be heard.

We're not taught how to take space gently.

We think it has to mean pulling away.

We think needing time alone means something is broken.

We treat silence like distance and boundaries like rejection.

But space, real, honest, intentional space, is an act of trust.

It says:

"I know our connection is strong enough to stretch without snapping."

"I know I can take a step back and still find you when I return."

"I know I'm allowed to be whole on my own, even while I love you."

This kind of space doesn't close the door.

It simply opens a window.

The need for space can arise in many forms.

Sometimes you need physical distance, a night alone, a walk by yourself, a weekend to recharge.

Sometimes it's emotional, time to process your thoughts without translating them into conversation.

Sometimes it's energetic, a pause from the constant exchange of feelings, so you can find your own again.

Whatever the form, the need is valid.

It's not a betrayal of the bond.

It's an honoring of your capacity.

Because staying close without rest eventually turns closeness into pressure.

And pressure, left unchecked, becomes resentment.

There's a difference between withdrawing and restoring.

Withdrawing says: *I can't do this.*

Restoring says: *I want to keep doing this, but I need time to come back to myself first.*

When both people can recognize that difference, space becomes part of the rhythm, not an interruption.

It becomes something you can speak about.

Something you can ask for without guilt.

Something you can receive without fear.

And the result?

Closeness that doesn't suffocate.

Connection that lasts longer because it's allowed to breathe.

You learn how to take space without vanishing.

You send the message that says, "I need a quiet night, but I'm thinking of you."

You turn off your phone without shutting the door.

You spend the day on your own, but return with more to give.

This is the art of healthy distance.

Not fueled by avoidance.

Not driven by fear.

But shaped by self-awareness and respect.

You leave, *and come back better.*

You step away, *and the bond deepens, not disappears.*

Because love that honors autonomy grows stronger, not weaker.

Sometimes it's not about asking for space, it's about recognizing when someone else needs it.

They grow quieter.

They stop initiating.

They seem a little more inward.

And the instinct may be to reach, to pull, to question.

But sometimes, the most loving thing you can do is *step back with softness.*

To let them drift without interpreting it as disinterest.

To trust their rhythm.

To stay present without pressing.

It's not easy.

But it's generous.

And generosity, in this case, looks like patience.

Space doesn't mean you love each other less.

Sometimes it means you love each other so much, you want to preserve the connection instead of wearing it out.

You want to come back to it with fresh eyes, a rested heart, and a fuller self.

And sometimes, it's in the distance that you remember just how much it matters.

You feel their absence in the places they usually fill.

You miss their voice, not because they've left, but because you stepped into quiet by choice.

You realize the weight of their presence, not as burden, but as *comfort*.

And that realization returns you to them with deeper appreciation.

Closeness thrives when it's chosen, not just once, but over and over.

And to keep choosing someone, you have to stay connected to yourself.

You have to make room for your own thoughts.

You have to let your body rest in its own rhythm.

You have to remember what *your* voice sounds like without the echo of another always beside it.

This is how you remain whole.

So that when you do return, you bring a full self to the relationship, not just a role.

And when both people do this, the space between them becomes charged with care.

Not tension.

Not fear.

Care.

Space can feel like silence, and silence can feel like uncertainty.

Especially when you're used to talking every day.

When presence has become a kind of rhythm.

When closeness feels like your default.

The sudden shift, the quiet, can stir up questions.

Did I say something wrong?

Are they pulling away?

Is this the beginning of distance that won't close again?

It's natural to feel this.

To wonder, to doubt, to reach.

But sometimes, the silence doesn't mean separation.

It means they're listening inward.

It means they're making room for their own thoughts.

And if you can trust that, if you can let the stillness be a part of the connection, it becomes less threatening, more meaningful.

Sometimes the space you need is from the *us,* so you can return to the *me.*

You've been so woven into the relationship, into the shared decisions and combined routines, that your own preferences get quiet.

Not erased.

Just... paused.

And one day you realize:

You're not sure what you want to do with your free time.

You don't remember the last thing you did *just for yourself.*

You miss your own mind.

That realization doesn't mean the relationship is broken.

It means you're ready to restore your edges.

To reintroduce yourself to yourself, so you can keep offering your wholeness to the other person.

In a healthy relationship, there's room for two full people.

Not one absorbing the other.

Not one orbiting the other.

But two centers.

Two lives.

Two rhythms that keep choosing to move in sync, even as they remain distinct.

And that distinction, that sovereignty, is what allows the connection to breathe.

Without it, even love becomes suffocating.

We often confuse closeness with constant access.

But love doesn't mean being available at all hours.

It doesn't mean responding instantly.

It doesn't mean filling every silence or smoothing every edge.

Sometimes love looks like:

"I'll respond when I've had a moment to breathe."

"I need today for myself, but I'll see you tomorrow."

"I care about you deeply, and I'm also tending to me."

This isn't withdrawal.

It's maturity.

A kind of love that's steady because it isn't desperate.

That gives because it isn't depleted.

The need for space can come even in moments of joy.

You've had a beautiful stretch of time together.

Laughter, ease, affection.

And then, the impulse to be alone.

Not because anything's wrong.

But because fullness asks for pause.

You want to sit in your own skin again.

To integrate what you've felt.

To stretch back out into your own dimensions.

When closeness is real, it gives you permission for that pause.

It doesn't panic.

It doesn't guilt.

It understands:

Space after connection isn't abandonment.

It's absorption.

It's the moment you make meaning out of presence.

There are also times when space isn't something you ask for, it's something that happens naturally.

One of you gets busy.

A trip, a project, a shift in energy.

The contact slows.

The conversations lag.

The pattern changes.

And in the quiet, you find yourself reaching inward.

You don't feel abandoned.

You just feel *alone*, and sometimes, that's necessary.

Because solitude reorients you.

It reminds you that you're not just someone's partner or person, you're
you.

And being *you* fully is the only way to be part of something fully.

Sometimes the bravest thing you can do in love is step back.

Not to leave.

Not to test.

But to trust.

To let the relationship breathe without your constant tending.

To give the other person the dignity of their own space.

To give yourself the same.

This is a higher kind of closeness.

Not based on control.

Not based on dependency.

But on choice, continuously renewed.

Not because of proximity.

But because of presence, even when you're apart.

Space doesn't have to mean distance.

It can be gentle.

It can be kind.

It can be something you offer one another as a form of rest.

A breath.

A margin.

A stillness between the beats.

Think of it like music:

Without the rests, the notes lose meaning.

Without the pauses, the rhythm has no pulse.

Space gives shape to sound.

To feeling.

To love.

It says: "This is where we pause so that we can keep going."

There may be moments when space brings up old fears.

Memories of people who left.

Times when distance did mean disconnection.

Stories where love faded the moment things got quiet.

It's okay to feel those echoes.

But don't let them dictate the present.

Every connection is different.

And the ones that last are often the ones that make room for everything, even the need to step away.

Because stepping away isn't always a sign of slipping.

Sometimes it's the very thing that makes return possible.

Space gives you perspective.

You remember how to look at the relationship from the outside, not because you want out, but because you want to see it clearly.

You remember who you are when you're not immersed in the shared rhythm.

You hear your own thoughts more loudly.

You sit with your own feelings without rushing to translate them into dialogue.

And sometimes, in that quiet, you realize things you couldn't inside the closeness.

What you want.

What you need.

What you miss, not because it's absent, but because it's yours to return to more fully.

You can love someone deeply and still need air.

You can be completely committed and still crave aloneness.

Still crave your own bed.

Still crave an evening without conversation or compromise.

This doesn't make you selfish.

It makes you honest.

It means you value the relationship enough to protect your own clarity.

To stay centered enough to keep showing up well.

To not let love turn into a blur where your sense of self dissolves.

Because proximity without pause eventually exhausts everyone.

And closeness that denies individuality can't sustain itself.

Sometimes space isn't just about restoration.

It's about remembering.

You remember that you are more than how you relate.

More than how you're loved.

More than who you are with them.

You are a story before and after this bond.

And honoring that story, keeping it alive, nurturing it, helps you bring a fuller version of yourself into the relationship.

This is how space becomes meaningful:

Not as absence, but as integration.

Not as disconnection, but as realignment.

You don't leave to escape.

You leave to return, differently, more fully, more rooted.

The hardest spaces to take are the ones we didn't expect to need.

You're in a season of ease.

Things feel good.

You're grateful, settled, connected.

And yet, you feel a tug.

The desire to step back.

To quiet the shared energy.

To listen to yourself again.

It's confusing, even guilt-inducing.

Why now?

Why distance when everything feels right?

But this is what many of us never learned:

Needing space doesn't mean something's wrong.

Sometimes, needing space is exactly what keeps everything *right*.

You begin to trust your inner signals more.

Not every urge for solitude is a red flag.

Not every pause is a precursor to a problem.

Not every quiet day means you're drifting apart.

You learn to tell the difference between isolation and introspection.

Between pulling away and pulling inward.

Between shutting down and tuning in.

And when both people in a relationship can recognize those differences, something beautiful happens:

Space becomes part of the connection, not a break from it.

It becomes a shared understanding.

A rhythm you both respect.

A way of loving each other with room to breathe.

There's a different kind of closeness that forms when space is allowed.

It's less fragile.

Less reactive.

Less afraid.

Because it knows it doesn't have to grip to hold on.

It knows that stepping away doesn't mean vanishing.

It knows that love can stretch, and flex, and still stay intact.

This kind of love doesn't require constant reassurance.

Because it's built on trust, not transaction.

It allows you to return, not to prove your loyalty, but because you *want* to.

Because the space you took reminded you how much the connection matters.

You might find yourself missing them in unexpected ways.

Not dramatically.

Not urgently.

But in the little quiet corners of your day.

You think of the way they always stretch first thing in the morning.

Or the way they rest their head against yours in silence.

Or the way they hum when they're cooking and don't realize you're watching.

These aren't desperate memories.

They're warm ones.

They soften the distance.

They remind you why you're coming back.

And they prove that space doesn't erase affection, it often reveals it.

Healthy distance leads to healthy return.

You come back to each other with more patience.

With more gratitude.

With a fresh perspective on the shared space between you.

The things that used to grate at you feel smaller now.

The things you appreciated, but overlooked, feel brighter.

It's not that time apart solves everything,

It just refreshes the lens.

It lets you see each other not through the fog of habit, but through the clarity of choice.

I still choose you.

I still want to be here.

I still love this, not out of routine, but because I've remembered its value.

Space doesn't just help us grow individually.

It helps the relationship evolve.

It shows you where the edges are.

Where you both hold tension.

Where communication needs work.

Where you feel free, and where you still feel confined.

It invites honest conversation, not just about your connection, but about your own emotional ecology.

What do I need to stay present?

Where do I lose myself too easily?

What kind of silence helps me listen better?

When space is honored, it becomes a mirror.

And from that reflection, intimacy deepens.

Not just because you *reconnect*,

but because you *know yourselves better* when you do.

Sometimes the deepest act of love is stepping back with care.

Not out of frustration.

Not to prove a point.

But to honor the truth that even the strongest connection needs lightness.

Needs room.

Needs air.

You feel the instinct to lean in, to hold on, to explain, to stay close, and instead, you pause.

You take a breath.

You give them space.

You give yourself space.

And that pause, that breath, becomes a quiet offering.

A way of saying, *I trust the bond enough to not press against it constantly.*

This doesn't mean you withdraw emotionally.

It means you step back physically, energetically, or conversationally, with respect.

You learn to give space *with love still intact.*

You soften your reach.

You let the silence stretch without trying to solve it.

You hold your presence like an open hand, not a clenched fist.

And what returns to you in those moments is clarity, not control.

You begin to see what's truly yours to carry and what's not.

You learn what belongs to their process.

You learn to witness without managing, to support without fixing.

This is mature closeness.

Not based on proximity, based on permission.

In the most grounded relationships, space is built into the foundation.

You don't need a crisis to ask for time alone.

You don't need to manufacture tension to justify rest.

It's understood:

We will love better if we take care of our own minds, hearts, and bodies first.

We will connect more fully if we don't demand from each other what we can only give ourselves.

We will stay close longer if we don't make closeness the measure of safety.

Because true intimacy doesn't collapse when you take a step back.

It remembers its shape.

And waits, patiently, for the return.

There will be moments when space feels harder than closeness.

When the silence stretches longer than expected.

When you wonder if you've given too much room.

When doubt creeps in and says, *What if they don't come back?*

These moments are part of the rhythm too.

And in them, you practice something deeper than control, you practice *faith*.

Not blind hope.

Not naivety.

But trust rooted in the pattern of the relationship you've built.

Trust that the foundation can hold.

Trust that their return, when it comes, will be honest, not forced.

Trust that even if things shift, you will still be okay.

Space teaches you to hold yourself more gently.

You stop assigning urgency to every feeling.

You stop expecting someone else to constantly stabilize your inner world.

You begin to soothe your own nervous system.

You begin to reconnect to your breath, your thoughts, your intentions.

This is not a retreat from love.

It's a return to self.

And in that return, something softens.

You realize that the strongest relationships are made of two people who know how to be alone, and still choose to walk together.

Not out of need.

But out of desire.

Out of mutual respect.

Out of earned trust.

The more space you take with care, the more you come to value the quiet parts of connection.

Not the declarations.

Not the celebrations.

But the steady return.

The way someone re-enters your day without fanfare.

The way their voice shows up again like a song you hadn't realized you missed.

These are the moments that prove love isn't measured only by presence.

It's also measured by the grace with which we let each other go, and the peace with which we let each other come back.

It's easy to believe that taking space means growing apart.

But sometimes, the opposite is true.

Space reveals what's real.

What holds without being held.

What stays in the absence of effort.

What deepens even when nothing is being said.

When you allow for space and find that the connection still lives, still breathes, you're no longer just holding onto each other.

You're holding *with* each other.

That's the kind of love that lasts.

Because it trusts the strength of what's been built.

Even in the quiet.

Even in the stretch.

Even when everything in you wants to close the gap faster.

You can feel someone's care even in their absence.

In the way they honor your boundary.

In the way they don't demand a timeline.

In the way they leave the door open without knocking every hour.

This kind of respect is rare.

And when you receive it, you remember what healthy love sounds like.

It doesn't rush.

It doesn't guilt.

It doesn't force presence to prove worth.

It allows the relationship to rest when needed, because what's real can handle the pause.

When you finally return, when the space has served its purpose, it doesn't always look like a grand reunion.

Sometimes, it's simple.

A message.

A glance.

A hand reaching back across a shared table.

And in that gesture is everything:

The trust that held.

The patience that waited.

The connection that stretched but never snapped.

You settle in beside them, and something in you exhales.

Not because the space was easy, but because it was honored.

And anything honored becomes stronger.

Eventually, you learn how to hold space, not just for yourself, but for each other.

You stop rushing to fill the silence.

You stop interpreting every pause as a problem.

You start to listen for what isn't being said, and you give it room to arrive when it's ready.

This is what deep love looks like over time:

A kind of patience.

A kind of peace.

You're not afraid of space anymore.

You've seen what it gives back.

You begin to realize that distance doesn't always mean danger.

Sometimes it's devotion, expressed in a different language.

The devotion that says, *I'd rather wait for the whole you than keep only a piece.*

The devotion that says, *I'll stay here, not chasing, not demanding, but holding the door open when you're ready to come in.*

And when that door swings back open,

when the return happens without pressure, without urgency, but with *presence,*

you feel the quiet miracle of a connection that can stretch and still hold.

The space between two people becomes its own kind of container.

A place where emotions breathe.

Where identities stay distinct.

Where the relationship grows not through constant contact, but through rhythm, balance, and respect.

You stop needing to fill every moment.

You stop fearing what a little distance might mean.

Instead, you use it.

To reflect.

To renew.

To come back with clearer eyes and a softer presence.

Because love, when nurtured like this, doesn't wear down.

It expands.

You no longer ask, "How can we avoid space?"

You begin to ask better questions:

"How can we honor it when it comes?"

"How can we let it serve us, rather than scare us?"

"How can we learn to pause *without losing each other?*"

These questions create a new kind of closeness.

One that doesn't cling.

One that doesn't crumble.

One that doesn't vanish at the first sign of separation.

Because now you both know:

You're not here because of proximity.

You're here because of *choice.*

And choice makes every return a little more meaningful.

There's a powerful kind of love that says:

"I trust you enough to take your space."

"I trust us enough to let things breathe."

"I trust myself enough to stand in the quiet and not panic."

This kind of love takes practice.

And it takes people who are willing to stop proving, and start *being.*

Being still.

Being honest.

Being present, even in the spaces where nothing is being exchanged.

And that presence, when it's felt, speaks louder than constant closeness ever could.

The greatest closeness doesn't erase space.

It honors it.

It learns how to sit beside someone who needs room.

It learns how to say, "Take your time," and mean it.

It learns how to stay connected, even when contact is minimal.

This is how you build a bond that doesn't shrink when stretched.

That doesn't demand to be fed constantly.

That grows in the gaps as much as in the overlaps.

Because now you know:

It's not how close you are every moment that matters.

It's how you hold the *moments between.*

There's a moment, after a long stretch of quiet, when you reach for each other again.

Not from panic.

Not from guilt.

Just from the natural tug of return.

And when it happens, something deep inside settles.

You remember:

We're still here.

This is still ours.

Space didn't take it away, it gave us back to ourselves, and now we're giving that fullness back to each other.

You speak more gently.

You listen more openly.

You touch with awareness, not just affection.

Because everything means a little more when you've chosen it after the stillness.

Closeness is easy to measure when you're together.

But the real strength of a bond is seen in the quiet times.

When things go unsaid but are still understood.

When time apart doesn't unnerve you.

When space is seen not as separation, but as a necessary element of growth.

The strongest relationships are not the ones with the most shared hours, but the ones that know how to stretch without snapping.

That know how to rest without disappearing.

That know how to love without needing to constantly *hold*.

Because sometimes, the most loving hands… are the ones that let go gently.

Space, it turns out, is not the opposite of love.

It is part of its language.

It says:

"I will not rush your process."

"I will not interrupt your inner world."

"I will not forget you just because you're quiet."

And that kind of spacious love, the kind that holds steady, quietly, through days of distance or introspection, is the kind that heals.

It doesn't panic.

It doesn't punish.

It waits, openly.

Because it's rooted not in possession, but in presence.

And presence, once established, doesn't disappear in the pause.

It *remains*.

Chapter 8: Apart Again

No matter how close you become to someone, there will come a day when you are apart.

Sometimes it's temporary.

Sometimes it's chosen.

Sometimes it arrives without your permission.

But it always leaves a mark.

Because once you've known real closeness, the kind that lives in the body, the kind that rewrites how you move through the world, its absence is not a blank space.

It's a presence in reverse.

You don't just notice what's gone.

You feel what *used* to be there.

And that's a different kind of ache entirely.

The room feels different.

The air quieter, heavier.

Your habits persist, setting out two mugs instead of one, reaching for your phone to text them before remembering there's nothing to say right now.

It's not just about missing someone.

It's about *adjusting to their absence*.

About trying to make sense of space that used to be filled.

About discovering how much of your day was built around them, not in dependency, but in rhythm.

And now that rhythm falters.

The beat is off.

The silence is louder than sound.
You try to keep moving.
You go about your day.
You laugh with other people.
You check your calendar, clean your space, finish your work.
And still,
They hover.
Not as a distraction, but as a *shadow presence*.
Not painful, not always, just... constant.
You feel them in the stretch between moments.
You remember them in the way you now sit alone.
And suddenly, you understand that separation isn't a moment, it's an *adjustment*.
One you make again and again.
There are different kinds of absence.
Some are sharp, like a door slammed shut.
Some are slow, like fog rolling in.
Sometimes the person is gone physically, but still lingers emotionally.
Sometimes they're nearby, but the closeness has shifted.
Sometimes you both drift, not because you want to, but because life pulled in different directions.
And what's hardest is that there's often no single point of clarity.
No conclusion.
Just a gradual realization that something that used to feel near... now does not.
And you're left to figure out what to do with the space they leave behind.
Grief isn't only for death.
It's for all the forms of departure.
The friend who no longer texts first.
The partner who moved to another city.
The family member who grows quieter with every phone call.
The version of someone you once knew, before time, before tension, before change.

You grieve what was.

You grieve what still lives in memory.

You grieve what might have been, if the timeline had bent differently.

And the grief is strange,

because it's not always loud.

Sometimes it's just a dull ache.

A weight in your chest at midnight.

A thought you can't finish because it reminds you too much of them.

You might find yourself reaching for them in small, habitual ways.

Scrolling through photos.

Typing a message and not sending it.

Bringing up their name in conversation even when it hurts.

It's not weakness.

It's *memory in motion.*

You're trying to hold onto what connection gave you.

You're trying to keep some thread alive.

And sometimes that thread is what gets you through the day.

Even if it's frayed.

Even if it only exists in your mind.

Some days you'll feel fine.

You'll laugh genuinely.

You'll feel light, even free.

You'll start to imagine what's next, not just what was.

And then,

a song, a scent, a phrase someone says, and there they are.

Suddenly in the room again.

Suddenly in your chest again.

And just like that, you're back in it.

Longing.

Remembering.

Wishing they were here to witness something simple, something small, something meaningful only because they're the one who would've understood.

This is the hard truth: closeness rewires you.

Once someone has lived in your thoughts, in your body, in your days, their absence is not an undoing.

It's a *repatterning*.

You have to learn how to think without looping back to them.

How to walk through familiar places and not expect to see them.

How to come home to yourself again, slowly, without their echo always following.

This doesn't mean forgetting.

It doesn't mean erasing.

It means healing with the imprint still intact.

Longing isn't always a sign to return.

Sometimes it's just part of the cost of connection.

You let someone in, deeply.

They became part of you.

And now they're not here in the same way.

That doesn't mean it was wrong.

That doesn't mean it's over.

That doesn't mean it's broken.

It means you are human.

Capable of deep presence.

And, therefore, capable of deep ache.

This is not weakness.

This is evidence of how much love mattered.

Sometimes what hurts most is not what's said, but what's left unsaid.

The message you didn't send.

The moment you didn't know would be the last.

The goodbye that was more of a fade-out than a full stop.

You keep replaying scenes in your head, trying to trace where the connection began to loosen.

Was it that conversation?

That silence?

That stretch of days when neither of you reached out?

There's no clear answer.

Just an ache that says: something meaningful has gone quiet.

And now you're left holding the echo.

There's a difference between being alone and being *without someone*.

Alone can be peaceful.

Alone can be chosen.

But "without" carries the weight of memory.

You walk into a place and remember how they moved through it.

You hear a song and remember the exact way they sang along.

You say something you know would've made them laugh, and the silence that follows feels louder than sound.

This is the landscape of separation:

Everything familiar, altered.

Everything ordinary, touched by the ghost of closeness.

You might try to distract yourself.

New habits.

New people.

New places.

And sometimes it works, for a little while.

But then you realize that healing isn't about replacing.

It's about making peace with the space they left behind.

Not filling it.

Not rushing past it.

But sitting inside it long enough to hear what it has to say.

Grief isn't a detour from the journey.

It *is* the journey, the part that softens you, strips you, reshapes you.

And teaches you, above all, that real connection always leaves a trace.

The longing doesn't mean you want to go back.

Sometimes it just means you miss who you were with them.

The ease.

The softness.

The way they saw you, clearly, kindly, in a season when you needed it.

You're not clinging to the past.

You're honoring it.

Because some relationships aren't meant to last forever, but they *are* meant to mark you.

And what they give you doesn't disappear just because they're gone.

There's an ache in knowing they still exist, they're just no longer part of your everyday life.

They're out there.

Maybe thriving.

Maybe struggling.

Maybe missing you too, or maybe not at all.

You'll never fully know.

And that's its own kind of grief,

the grief of unfinished knowing.

The grief of parallel lives that once intersected so vividly... now moving forward on separate paths.

No anger.

No closure.

Just distance, lived and accepted.

You start to carry their absence more quietly.

At first it felt sharp, invasive, constant.

But over time, it becomes part of the background.

Still there.

Still felt.

But no longer shouting.

You learn to live around the empty space.

To laugh while still holding sorrow.

To reach for joy without waiting for it to erase the ache.

This is the maturity of separation:

Not that it stops hurting, but that it stops *consuming.*

You hurt *and* you continue.

You long *and* you grow.

You remember *and* you live.

Sometimes, being apart reveals things that closeness concealed.

You see your own patterns more clearly.

You notice what you gave too easily.

You understand what wasn't sustainable, even if it was beautiful.

You begin to separate the love from the dynamic.

To hold onto what was true without holding onto what was painful.

To admit what didn't work while still cherishing what did.

This is the gift of distance:

Not always clarity, but *perspective*.

And from that perspective, healing begins.

You stop measuring your healing by how often you think of them.

You know better now.

You understand that memories will return,

in flashes, in dreams, in quiet hours.

And they're not a setback.

They're just visits.

A part of you remembering what mattered.

A part of you honoring your own capacity to care deeply.

And eventually, those visits stop hurting.

Eventually, they begin to feel... soft.

Not sweet.

Not bitter.

Just real.

Proof that you lived something that mattered, even if it didn't stay.

You might wonder if they miss you, too.

If your name ever still catches in their throat.

If your laugh still echoes in their memory.

If they ever think of texting you, and don't.

And maybe they do.

Maybe they don't.

But either way, you learn that your worth is not tied to their memory of you.

You were real.

You were kind.

You showed up with your heart.

And that's enough, even if they never say it out loud.

Even if they never come back.

There's a point in every kind of loss where you stop expecting them to come back.

Not because you've given up.

But because something in you accepts that what was, *is no longer.*

The waiting softens.

The checking quiets.

The ache settles into something less sharp, more woven into your day.

You no longer listen for their footsteps.

You no longer pause at your phone hoping it lights up.

You simply... continue.

Not out of numbness.

But out of resilience.

You've learned to live around the absence.

To let it be a part of your landscape, not the whole story.

Some people leave your life, and the world doesn't pause to let you process.

You still have to make breakfast.

Still have to show up to work.

Still have to respond to messages, run errands, be polite, get things done.

But behind every task, there's a weight you're carrying that others can't see.

This is the loneliness of invisible grief:

The kind where nothing looks broken on the outside.

But inside, you're rearranging everything.

Figuring out how to keep moving without what once moved with you.

And some days, that effort, just *continuing*, is the most courageous thing you do.

Eventually, you stop trying to "get over" them.

You stop chasing closure as a finish line.

You stop treating healing like a race.

You realize that love doesn't need to be undone to be released.

It just needs to be honored, and then slowly re-shelved.

Not discarded.

Not denied.

Just... placed gently in the back of your mind, where it can rest without ruling you.

This is where healing shifts.

From forgetting, to remembering differently.

From resistance, to acceptance.

From ache, to quiet acknowledgment.

One of the strangest parts of losing someone emotionally is how your instincts keep reaching for them long after they're gone.

You hear a piece of news and think, *I should tell them.*

You laugh at a joke and instinctively imagine their reaction.

You go to say their name and stop yourself, not because it hurts, but because it no longer fits the moment.

It's not that you've erased them.

It's that your life is slowly reshaping around the absence.

And the places where they once lived are no longer center-stage.

They're still there.

Just quieter now.

Not all separation is painful.

Sometimes, with enough time and perspective, it becomes... tender.

You look back with a kind of fondness.

Not because it ended well, maybe it didn't, but because you can finally hold the memory without tightening your jaw.

You see them for what they were:

A chapter.

A mirror.

A necessary moment in your becoming.

They didn't complete you.

They *revealed* you.

And even if you never speak again, something in you says:

Thank you for what we were. Even if that's all we'll ever be.

136

There's a softness in making peace with someone's absence.
Not passive.
Not resigned.
But gentle.
Still.
You stop needing answers they'll never give.
You stop waiting for apologies that may never arrive.
You stop editing the story, trying to rewrite what already happened.
You just let it be what it was.
Beautiful.
Messy.
Incomplete.
And enough.
Not because it was perfect.
But because it shaped you.
And growth, even through pain, is always enough.
Sometimes, the most important person in your life becomes a stranger again.
Not out of anger.
Not out of loss.
But out of time.
Life continues.
Their path winds in another direction.
Yours does too.
And slowly, without even realizing it, you stop knowing their details.
Their favorite coffee changes.
Their laugh evolves.
Their world moves, and you are no longer a part of it.
It's not betrayal.
It's life.
Still, that realization lands quietly.
A soft closing of a door that was left cracked open, just in case.
There will always be reminders.

Objects.

Songs.

Phrases.

Corners of your world they once inhabited.

You don't need to remove them.

You just learn how to live beside them differently.

What used to hurt becomes familiar.

What used to sting becomes neutral.

What used to take your breath away now makes you exhale.

This is how memory matures.

It doesn't fade, it transforms.

You no longer need it to feel anything specific.

You just let it be part of you, without needing it to change you anymore.

You'll meet people who help you hold the ache.

Not by fixing it.

Not by replacing the person who's gone.

But by seeing it, and not running.

They don't flinch when you talk about the past.

They don't panic when you get quiet.

They don't compete with your history.

They just stay.

Present.

Open.

Willing to know you as you are, including what you've lost.

These people become part of the healing.

Not because they fill the space.

But because they sit beside it with you.

And in that shared presence, something slowly repairs.

There's a strange moment, after enough time has passed, when you realize you're no longer waiting.

Not for a message.

Not for a reason.

Not for closure.

Just... not waiting.

You've stepped back into your life.

Into your skin.

Into your days without checking the rearview mirror.

You don't know the exact moment it happened, the shift from longing to living,

but you feel it.

The ache isn't gone.

But it's no longer in charge.

And that, quietly, feels like freedom.

You begin to see how the loss shaped you, not just emotionally, but relationally.

How it taught you to listen better.

How it showed you your boundaries.

How it revealed where you disappear too easily, and where you hold on too tightly.

Separation, if you let it, becomes a kind of mirror.

It shows you your own patterns in clearer light.

Not to shame you.

But to inform you.

So that the next time you love,

you do it with more intention.

More presence.

More care.

Not because you're afraid of losing again,

but because you've learned how to hold without gripping.

You don't always talk about them anymore.

Not because you've forgotten.

But because the story has moved.

It's no longer the centerpiece of your conversations.

It's no longer the pulse behind every pause.

It's something true, but past.

Something meaningful, but finished.

And when their name does come up, it feels like dust in sunlight.
Still visible.
Still moving.
But no longer heavy.
Healing is not linear, you've learned this by now.
You'll be fine for weeks.
And then one ordinary morning, something catches you off guard.
A scent.
A line from a book.
The sight of a jacket that looks like one they used to wear.
And suddenly, it's all there again.
Not in full force, but enough to make you pause.
Enough to remind you:
You cared. Deeply. And care leaves a trace.
You don't spiral anymore.
You don't shut down.
You just let the feeling move through.
And then, you move too.
There's a kind of clarity that only distance can offer.
Not the forced kind, the kind that arrives gently, once the noise has settled.
You see things differently now.
What you compromised too quickly.
What you feared too deeply.
What you wanted so badly that you overlooked what wasn't working.
You don't hate yourself for it.
You don't blame them either.
You simply see.
And from that seeing, you begin to grow in a direction that's more aligned
with the truth of who you are now.
Time teaches you how to reframe the ending.
You stop labeling it as failure.
You stop asking what you should've done differently.
You stop holding it like a wound that won't close.

Instead, you begin to honor it like a chapter.

It had its beginning.

Its beauty.

Its lessons.

And yes, its end.

But endings, you realize, don't erase the worth of what came before.

They simply mark the place where something meaningful transformed, and made space for what's next.

You don't need to rebuild what you had in order to remember it with love.

You don't need reconciliation to validate that it mattered.

You don't need mutual understanding to carry forward your part of the story with grace.

You're allowed to outgrow the connection while still holding gratitude for what it gave you.

You're allowed to miss someone and not want them back.

You're allowed to feel peace and pain, in the same breath.

And one day, someone will ask you about them.

Not with judgment.

Not with pressure.

Just curiosity.

And you'll answer with a kind of calm you didn't expect.

You'll tell the truth, gently, maybe even fondly.

You'll mention the good.

The complicated.

The reasons it ended.

The things you'll always appreciate.

And when the conversation moves on, you won't feel hollow.

You'll feel whole.

Because this is what it means to heal:

Not to forget.

But to carry memory without being carried by it.

You may never fully understand what happened.

Why things faded.

Why the bond shifted.

Why you grew apart, even when it felt like you were growing together.

But you learn to stop demanding clarity from a past that can't offer more than it already has.

You learn that not everything unfinished is broken.

That not every goodbye needs an explanation.

That some stories are complete even without a final page.

And that peace doesn't always come from answers,

sometimes, it comes from *accepting that the questions no longer need to be asked.*

Eventually, you begin to carry them differently.

Not as weight.

Not as ache.

But as part of your story.

They become a memory you've made peace with.

A name that no longer stings.

A moment you no longer try to relive or rewrite.

And that peace doesn't mean indifference, it means growth.

It means you've learned to hold what was without needing it to become what is.

You stop hoping they'll reach out.

Not because it wouldn't mean something,

but because your life no longer depends on it.

You've filled your days again.

You've found laughter that doesn't echo with their absence.

You've built new rhythms, new rituals, new relationships.

Their silence no longer feels like a statement.

It just feels like part of the landscape,

something that used to speak, and now simply doesn't.

And you let it be quiet.

One day, you'll find yourself loving someone else.

Not in spite of the past, but shaped by it.

You'll recognize your own softness more clearly.

You'll know where your edges are.
You'll be more generous with time, more discerning with energy.
And when you feel fear, because you will,
it won't come from not knowing how to love again.
It'll come from knowing exactly how deeply you're capable of loving...
and choosing to open anyway.
That's the strength you carry forward.
Not guardedness, but wisdom.
Not armor, but intention.
You'll see them again, maybe.
At a distance.
In a dream.
Across a room.
On someone else's screen.
And you'll feel something, but it won't be longing.
It will be recognition.
A quiet nod from the past.
You'll think:
That was real.
That mattered.
That chapter closed, but it gave me something I'll always carry.
And then you'll return to your life,
still whole.
Still here.
Still capable of loving, again and again.
Some loves don't end.
They just change shape.
They move from presence to memory.
From daily interaction to internal dialogue.
From shared days to quiet gratitude.
You don't lose them.
You just lose the version of them that was yours for a while.
And in that letting go, you reclaim something important:

Yourself.
Your time.
Your energy.
Your forward motion.
You don't forget them,
but you stop trying to bring them with you.
And somehow, that's even more loving than holding on.
There will be moments when you still feel the distance.
When something aches.
When you remember something only they would understand.
You might reach for a song.
A journal.
A prayer.
Not to fix the feeling,
just to honor it.
Because feeling deeply isn't a flaw.
It's evidence of your aliveness.
And the ache?
That's not a weakness.
It's a reflection of how willing you were to show up in full.
The world keeps turning.
You make new plans.
You show up for new people.
You write new pages.
And bit by bit, the place they once occupied fills with other things.
Not in competition.
Not in replacement.
Just in *renewal.*
Your life becomes yours again.
Not as a return to how things were,
but as a new rhythm you've earned.
One that holds the past gently...
and still chooses to step into what's next.

This is how it happens:
One day, you don't think about them at all.
And when you realize that, it doesn't feel like betrayal, it feels like breath.
Like finally stepping outside after being indoors too long.
Like walking barefoot and feeling the earth hold you.
Like remembering the sound of your own laughter, uninterrupted.
It's not victory.
It's not closure.
It's *aliveness*.
A return to your own rhythm.
Your own center.
Your own forward path.
Separation isn't always a loss.
Sometimes, it's a return.
To who you were.
To who you're becoming.
To the parts of yourself you'd set aside to make room for someone else.
You're not rebuilding.
You're rediscovering.
And what you find, after the ache, after the stillness, after the grief,
is that you've never stopped being whole.
Just changed.
Just stretched.
Just opened.
And now, even apart,
you're more together with yourself than you've ever been.

Chapter 9: The Return

C oming back to someone isn't always a grand event.
Sometimes, it's a quiet unfolding.
A glance held a little longer than usual.
A message sent after weeks of silence.
A moment that feels familiar, even though everything around it has changed.

Reconnection doesn't mean picking up exactly where you left off.

It means arriving, again, with new eyes, a fuller heart, and a deeper understanding of what distance taught you.

The return is not about reliving what was.

It's about discovering what's still true.

Returning is not always romantic.

Sometimes it's the friend you stopped talking to.

Sometimes it's the sibling you grew apart from.

Sometimes it's a version of yourself you lost somewhere along the way.

And the return is not dramatic.

It's subtle.

A softened tone.

A door reopened.

A willingness to speak honestly, maybe for the first time in a long time.

Because what matters most in returning is not the speed.

It's the sincerity.

You're not here to force things back.

You're here to see what still lives.

So much changes during distance.

You change.

They change.

Life reshapes both of you.

And when you meet again, however that happens, you bring those changes to the space between you.

You're not just reconnecting with who they were.

You're learning who they are now.

And you offer yourself the same way:

Not as a replica of your past self,

but as someone who's grown.

This is where return becomes powerful.

It's not a reset.

It's a reunion, rooted in what's real, not what was remembered.

The most honest returns are cautious.

Not cold.

Not guarded.

But careful, because care has been learned.

You know what it means to hurt.

You know what absence feels like.

You've lived in the ache, and you don't want to move without awareness now.

So you go slow.

You listen more.

You ask different questions.

You notice what feels steady, what feels rushed, what feels ready.

This is what makes reconnection strong.

Not urgency, but intention.

Sometimes, the return is mutual.

You both step forward, quietly, at the same time.

No rehearsed speeches.

No explanations demanded.

Just presence.

A recognition that even after all that time,
you still matter to each other.
It's not about fixing the past.
It's about offering the present with gentleness.
You sit across from each other and sense it,
a kind of relief.
The space is different now.
But the bond?
It's still there, waiting, patient, alive.
And sometimes, the return is one-sided.
You reach out.
You send the first message.
You take the risk.
And maybe they don't respond.
Or maybe they do, with hesitation, with limits, with questions.
This doesn't mean it wasn't worth trying.
Because the act of returning, of *offering* reconnection, is an act of hope.
An act of courage.
And whether or not it leads to what you imagined,
it tells the truth:
you cared enough to come back.
That matters.
Even if the chapter stays closed.
The return can also happen in layers.
First, a message.
Then, a call.
Then, a shared moment that feels a little like before, but steadier.
You don't try to collapse the space all at once.
You don't rush to reclaim every detail.
You build something new on the foundation of what once was.
And if it's going to last, it will grow slowly.
With boundaries.
With grace.

With curiosity.
Because real return is not just reunion, it's recalibration.
There's beauty in noticing what didn't change.
The sound of their laugh.
The way you finish each other's sentences.
The sense of ease that settles when you're both in the same room.
These things are gifts.
Not signs that nothing happened,
but proof that the core connection endured, even while you were apart.
And seeing that now, with fresh perspective,
is a reminder that some bonds don't break.
They just rest.
They go quiet.
They wait.
You'll feel tenderness during the return.
Not just toward them, but toward who you were when you first parted.
You'll remember how much you struggled to understand.
How much you hurt.
How much you grew in the silence.
And now, here you are.
Whole again.
Not because everything healed perfectly, but because *you kept going.*
This makes you softer.
More receptive.
More present.
Because return is not just reunion with another,
it's reconciliation with yourself.
Returning isn't about recreating the past.
It's about honoring what's still true now.
You don't come back to what *was*.
You come back to what *is*.
To who you are today.
To who they've become.

To the space that's been cleared, by time, by absence, by growth.

You don't pick up the pieces like nothing happened.

You acknowledge that something did.

And you build from there, gently.

Sometimes the return happens in silence before it happens in speech.

You think of them differently.

You feel less guarded.

You stop rehearsing what you'll say if you ever run into them again.

The energy shifts long before the conversation begins.

You soften toward them in your own thoughts.

You make room for the possibility that not every ending is final, and not every distance is permanent.

This quiet prelude is part of the process.

The heart making space before the body ever arrives.

The first few moments of reconnection can feel surreal.

You've imagined it so many times.

Planned your words.

Prepared your heart.

And now here you are, sitting across from them, hearing their voice again, watching their mannerisms resurface like nothing ever happened and everything has happened.

And in that moment, you realize:

You've both lived entire lives since you were last this close.

And still, something old and steady has survived the space.

Something warm.

Something familiar.

Something quietly glad to be back.

Return teaches you how to hold tension.

Because it's rarely simple.

You're happy to see them, but cautious.

You want to laugh, but you also want to understand.

You feel the joy of reunion, alongside the weight of everything that went unsaid.

And that's okay.

You don't need to resolve it all right now.

You don't need to fix every fracture in a single sitting.

You're allowed to let it unfold slowly.

You're allowed to revisit the past only as much as is helpful, and then leave it be.

Because return isn't about rehashing.

It's about renewing.

Sometimes, the return isn't dramatic or defining.

It's gradual.

A few texts.

A coffee catch-up.

A shared event.

And then, without anyone saying it aloud, you're just back in each other's lives.

Not always, not constantly.

But naturally.

This quiet re-entry can feel more grounding than any apology ever could.

Because it's not based in fixing.

It's based in showing up.

Again and again.

With no performance.

Just presence.

There's a humility that comes with returning.

You see where you misunderstood.

You see where you assumed.

You see where pain blocked your ability to listen.

And if they're doing the same, if they're arriving with their own clarity and care,

then something beautiful can grow in that mutual vulnerability.

Not the same as before.

Not a repeat.

Something new.

Something real.

Something chosen, again, and this time with full awareness of what that means.

You may find that some of what separated you no longer holds power.

The thing that felt like a wall now feels like a bump.

The difference that felt unbridgeable now feels like something you could hold with grace.

Because time didn't just change them.

It changed *you*.

And now, you're both better equipped to meet in the middle, not by becoming the same,

but by being more willing to understand each other's shape.

Return doesn't ask you to be different people.

It asks you to be *more whole*.

But not every return is permanent.

Some are brief.

A conversation.

A letter.

An hour of clarity between two lives that are still moving in different directions.

These returns matter too.

Because they close a loop.

Because they offer peace.

Because they let you say what you needed to say without demanding more.

Not all reconnection leads to reunion.

Sometimes it leads to release.

And that, too, is healing.

When return *is* lasting, it comes with new questions.

What does this look like now?

How do we protect what we've rebuilt?

What rhythms do we create that honor who we are now, not just who we were?

You stop trying to recover the old script.

You start writing a new one, together.

Not from nostalgia.

But from presence.

Not to erase the gap.

But to acknowledge it, and build something stronger because of it.

Because real return isn't just getting back.

It's *growing forward.*

The return doesn't erase the distance, it respects it.

It holds the space you both endured and doesn't try to shrink it or pretend it wasn't real.

You each carry what happened.

You each remember what it cost.

And now, you're here, not despite it, but *because of it.*

The ache, the silence, the reflection, it all brought you back differently.

And in this new version of closeness, there's no illusion that everything will be perfect.

But there *is* the quiet promise:

We're not starting over.

We're starting *from here.*

There's something tender in being chosen again.

Not because it's easy.

Not because you forgot what went wrong.

But because you *remember,* and you still chose this.

This is what trust rebuilt looks like.

It's not naive.

It's not blind.

It's aware, awake, intentional.

It says,

"I see what hurt us.

I see what nearly ended us.

And still, I believe there's more to write."

And maybe that belief isn't loud.

Maybe it's not even confident.

But it's steady.

And sometimes, steady is enough.

The return changes how you communicate.

You speak more clearly now.

You name things earlier.

You don't let silences stretch into assumptions.

You ask, "Are we okay?" not from fear, but from care.

You've lived without this connection.

You know what distance feels like.

And you don't want to drift again, not if you can help it.

So you check in more often.

You give fewer ultimatums and more invitations.

You own your part.

You listen better.

And in that mutual attention, something new forms, not just closeness, but *trust that's been tested.*

Return invites honesty about what needs to change.

You don't bring everything back with you.

Some patterns are left behind.

You let go of what no longer serves.

You name what's unsustainable.

You build new boundaries, not as barriers, but as containers for care.

This is not about control.

It's about capacity.

You're no longer trying to be everything to each other.

You're trying to be *what's true*, which is enough.

And in that space, you begin again, not smaller, but smarter.

Not heavier, but deeper.

You begin to see reconnection not as a gift from the past,

but as a vote for the future.

It's not about who you were.

It's about who you want to be, together, now.

This kind of return isn't a repeat.

It's a reveal.

A chance to uncover what was waiting beneath the noise.

A chance to walk the same path with more awareness, more patience, more grace.

You're not chasing magic.

You're tending to meaning.

And that, you've learned, is a more sustainable kind of love.

There's a tenderness that only exists between people who have known both closeness and distance.

You don't take the little things for granted anymore.

The check-in.

The shared glance.

The way they laugh at your old jokes like no time has passed.

You savor it.

Because now you know what absence feels like.

Now you know how quickly time can unravel what's not nurtured.

So you become more present.

Not out of fear, out of reverence.

You've been apart.

You've returned.

You *know* what this is worth.

Not every return is spoken.

Sometimes it's in the way they hold your hand differently.

The way they show up, on time, more fully, more consistently.

The way they ask, "How's your heart?" and really mean it.

These moments don't announce themselves.

But they say everything.

They say:

"I'm here."

"I've thought about this."

"I want this, still."

And you begin to relax again.

Not into old patterns, but into *new presence*.

Because this version of the relationship has nothing to prove,
only something to nurture.
Return makes you gentler with others, too.
You become more patient with misunderstandings.
More curious about silence.
More graceful with the people who are still finding their way back, to themselves, to others, to you.
You realize how fragile and brave reconnection can be.
And so you stop demanding immediate clarity.
You start holding space instead.
You start saying,
"It's okay.
Take your time.
I'm not going anywhere just yet."
And in that softness, others often find the courage to come closer.
The return doesn't guarantee permanence.
But it *does* offer possibility.
A chance to write a new ending.
Or a new chapter.
Or just a new moment that feels like peace.
And whatever shape it takes, however long it lasts,
you know it's real.
Because it came after the silence.
Because it came with intention.
Because it came without needing to be anything but *true*.
And sometimes, that's all you ever needed.
Sometimes, the most powerful part of the return isn't what's said, it's what's felt.
The unspoken ease.
The way their presence no longer stirs up tension.
The quiet recognition that you're both here because you *chose* to be.
No one begged.
No one pushed.

You just arrived, separately, wholly, and willingly.

And in that shared arrival, something soft and grounded begins to take root.

You realize this isn't about reclaiming what was lost.

It's about discovering what's possible now.

You find yourself smiling more.

Not because everything is perfect, but because you feel safer in the connection.

You trust the ground more.

You're not walking on memories, you're walking on new moments, new patterns, new care.

And it's not always loud.

It's the quiet texts that say, "Made it home safe."

The thoughtful check-ins.

The small, simple gestures that say, "I'm learning how to care for you better this time."

This is the return in action,

not dramatic, but *deliberate*.

Return is not just a moment.

It's a *practice*.

It's choosing to show up even when it feels awkward.

It's asking the hard questions and staying for the answers.

It's letting go of the urge to rewind, and embracing the mystery of what's next.

You wake up each day and decide again:

Yes, I'm still here.

Yes, I still want to learn how to love you well.

Yes, I'm willing to build something rooted in what's true *now*, not just what was beautiful *then*.

This kind of love takes presence.

And presence, once practiced, becomes powerfully sustaining.

There may still be moments of doubt.

You'll wonder:

Will we drift again?

Will the same things repeat?

Are we strong enough to carry this now?

And those questions are valid, they're human.

But this time, you ask them together.

You name the fear without hiding.

You speak to the tension before it turns to distance.

You commit not to never hurting each other, but to *repairing when it happens.*

This is the beauty of a mature return:

You don't promise perfection, you offer participation.

That's more honest.

And far more meaningful.

You start to feel the difference between being *close* and being *known.*

Before, maybe you shared space.

Now, you share understanding.

Before, you had connection.

Now, you have clarity.

You're not guessing how they feel.

You're not waiting for the other shoe to drop.

You talk.

You ask.

You listen, not to respond, but to *receive.*

And this, finally, is the kind of closeness you didn't even know you needed.

The kind that doesn't just fill the silence,

it honors it.

You stop trying to prove anything.

You're no longer trying to be easy to love.

You're no longer trying to shrink your needs to stay in the room.

You're no longer trying to keep everything light just to avoid the weight of honesty.

Because now, you know:

If this return is real, it can hold *all of you.*

CHAPTER 9: THE RETURN

The quiet.
The chaos.
The parts you used to hide just to be accepted.
And when they don't flinch, when they stay,
you realize something even deeper has returned:
Your trust.
Not just in them,
but in yourself, too.
Some returns aren't loud.
They're quiet rebuildings.
They happen in kitchens, folding laundry together.
On walks, without much said.
In long, slow conversations that begin with, "I've been thinking…"
And grow into something unshakable.
You begin to notice:
This isn't just about coming back to each other.
It's about coming back to *life together*.
One small shared task at a time.
One gentle offering at a time.
A steady rhythm.
A return to presence.
A kind of home you hadn't known you missed.
When you return, you begin to rewrite the story, not to erase the past, but
to give it new context.
You say things like:
"I didn't know how to handle that then."
"I thought I was protecting myself, but I was pushing you away."
"I'm sorry for what I didn't say."
And if you're both willing to hold those truths without defensiveness,
you build something new:
A deeper trust.
A wider understanding.
A place where neither of you has to be perfect to be safe.

This is how the return becomes restoration,

Not to the old form,

but to a stronger foundation.

You may find yourselves laughing again, not like before, but freer.

Because now, you're not pretending.

You're not performing.

You're not afraid that one wrong step will unravel everything.

You're more honest now.

More grounded.

More willing to hold the moment without clinging to it.

And in that freedom, joy returns too.

Not as escape,

but as presence.

Not as avoidance,

but as *evidence*.

That something has healed.

That something is alive.

That something is worth continuing.

At some point, you stop counting the time you spent apart.

Not because it didn't matter, but because what's being built now matters more.

You're not tracking days lost.

You're noticing days shared.

You're no longer measuring what could've been.

You're appreciating what *is*, even if it's quieter, slower, more deliberate.

Because this version of connection doesn't ask for proof.

It asks for presence.

It asks for care.

It asks for a new kind of courage, the courage to stay, gently.

There's peace in knowing that you didn't force the return.

That it came when it was ready.

That it came with reflection, not reaction.

That it came not because you couldn't be apart, but because you *chose* to come back together.

This makes everything feel sturdier.

More grounded.

More grown.

You're no longer clinging out of fear.

You're extending hands from a place of truth.

And that truth is simple:

"I still want this.

Even now.

Especially now."

You start to speak in new ways.

Less urgency.

More clarity.

Less guarding.

More truth.

You let your voice be soft, not because you're unsure, but because it no longer needs to be loud to be real.

You let your needs be known without apologizing.

You let theirs in without defensiveness.

And slowly, you co-create a space where both of you feel like you can *exhale*.

This is the return you didn't know you were waiting for:

The return to safety.

The return to shared breath.

The return to something that no longer feels fragile, only *alive*.

The past becomes something you can talk about without walking on eggshells.

You don't dissect every detail.

You don't rewrite the story.

You just honor it.

You say:

"This is what it was for me."

"This is how it felt then."

"This is what I've learned."
And they do the same.
Without blame.
Without shame.
Without trying to fix what's already gone.
You look at what was, and let it inform, not define, what is.
This is how return transforms the relationship:
It doesn't ignore the history.
It *includes* it, and still chooses forward.
You begin to dream together again.
Not in big, sweeping declarations.
But in small ways.
What should we cook next week?
Where do you want to go next summer?
What would it look like to make this feel even more like home?
These little questions are the seeds of a shared future.
Not because they're urgent, but because they're intentional.
You're not rushing.
You're not attaching outcome to every moment.
You're simply imagining together again.
And that imagination is the first sign of hope taking root.
Return teaches you to see love differently.
Not as constant presence.
Not as perfect understanding.
Not as always getting it right.
But as *returning*.
As circling back.
As staying curious.
As holding space for growth and change and renewal.
You stop needing the love to look a certain way.
You start trusting the *pattern* of showing up.
Because you know now:
What lasts isn't what never breaks.

It's what chooses to repair.
To rebuild.
To *return*.
Again and again, in small and steady ways.
You realize that what broke you open didn't end you.
It prepared you.
To receive.
To give.
To stay present when you would've once fled.
You've come through the silence.
You've come through the ache.
You've learned how to be okay on your own.
And now,
you're not returning because you *need* to be filled.
You're returning because you're full enough to share.
That changes everything.
Because now love is not a rescue, it's a *meeting place*.
Two whole selves.
Still learning.
Still choosing.
The most beautiful part of the return might be how normal it becomes.
The way they brush their hand against yours.
The way your name sounds again in their voice.
The way a familiar joke lands and laughter rises, effortless.
These aren't dramatic moments.
They're the small miracles of daily reconnection,
the evidence that something has not only resumed, but evolved.
That the bond didn't disappear, it deepened,
made more resilient by the distance it survived.
In the end, the return teaches you this:
Closeness isn't defined by how often you're together,
or how intensely you feel,
or how easily things unfold.

It's defined by your willingness to stay soft in the stretch.

To stay open in the uncertainty.

To keep choosing each other, not out of habit, but out of hope.

This is what real return looks like:

Not a restart.

Not a rescue.

A recognition.

I see you.

I've missed you.

And I'm still here.

Chapter 10: Closer Than Close

There comes a point in closeness when it stops feeling like something you *do*,
and starts feeling like something you simply *are*.

You no longer question the presence.

You no longer analyze every interaction.

You no longer need to reach, because the connection is already woven into your day.

This is a different kind of closeness.

Not loud.

Not urgent.

Not full of proof.

It's lived-in.

Steady.

Uncomplicated, not because it's shallow, but because it's settled.

This kind of closeness doesn't announce itself.

It shows up in the way you move around each other.

The way you share silence without trying to fill it.

The way you pause to look, really look, and realize you haven't been on guard in a while.

You've stopped performing.

You've stopped bracing.

You've let your body exhale, not just once, but often.

And now, the ease between you feels like part of the architecture.

Built over time.

Brick by brick.

Presence by presence.

There's a softness that comes with this stage.

Not because things are easy, but because they're familiar.

You know the shape of each other's rhythms.

You can feel when something's off without needing explanation.

You trust each other's space without fearing abandonment.

The questions that once felt like tests now feel like check-ins.

The disagreements that once felt threatening now feel navigable.

The silences that once felt loaded now feel safe.

Because you've learned that closeness isn't just about intensity.

It's about *continuity*.

Not what burns, but what stays.

You don't have to say, "I love you" every day for it to be true.

Now, the love shows up in smaller ways.

The second mug on the counter.

The pause in your voice when you ask how they're really doing.

The way you listen without planning your response.

These aren't romantic gestures.

They're relational ones.

The quiet kind of love that weaves itself into habit.

The kind that's easy to miss, until you realize how much it holds.

This is when closeness becomes your rhythm.

You don't think about the mechanics anymore.

You're not checking in on the bond constantly.

You're simply *living*, and they're part of the life you live.

You bring each other coffee.

You fold laundry while music plays.

You touch in passing and don't even realize how much it means.

And it means a lot.

Because closeness, at this stage, is not about confirming connection.

It's about *enjoying the presence* you've already built.

Without needing to explain it.

Without needing to protect it.
Just living in it.
There's a peace that comes when someone becomes familiar,
not in the sense of routine, but in the sense of *being known*.
You don't wonder how they'll react to your moods.
You don't feel the need to translate every emotion.
You don't fear that a bad day will make them question your bond.
Instead, you move honestly.
You let the rough edges show.
And they stay, not out of obligation, but out of understanding.
This is when you realize:
you're no longer managing closeness.
You're *resting in it*.
You share silence not as a void, but as a presence.
You cook side by side without speaking.
You sit in the same room doing separate things,
and somehow, that feels more connected than conversation ever could.
Because it's not about constant engagement.
It's about emotional proximity,
the kind that doesn't need attention to be real.
You can feel each other, even in the quiet.
You can sense each other, even in stillness.
And this knowing, this quiet thread between you,
becomes more comforting than words ever were.
You stop keeping score.
Not because everything is even,
but because it no longer matters.
You're not measuring love in acts or effort.
You're not balancing the emotional checkbook.
You trust the flow.
You trust that they care.
You trust that you care,
and that, together, you'll keep showing up.

Not because of duty.

Because it feels right.

Because it feels *real*.

Because closeness has become a shared rhythm,

not a shared performance.

Eventually, you realize that the love has matured into something *unshakable*.

Not unbreakable, you've lived enough to know that anything can change.

But unshakable, because it's not built on fantasy.

It's built on presence.

On acceptance.

On the repeated choice to be here, just as you are.

You don't need them to save you.

They don't need you to complete them.

You just meet, fully.

And in that meeting, the relationship feels whole.

You know you're closer than close when presence no longer feels fragile.

You don't wake up wondering if they'll stay.

You don't filter your words to keep the peace.

You don't shrink your needs in fear of being too much.

Instead, you live, wholly, openly, and their closeness *supports* that.

It doesn't ask you to change to keep it.

It asks you to *be*, and promises to meet you there.

This kind of love doesn't orbit around performance.

It rests in permission.

You begin to recognize the subtle ways they've become part of you.

Not in the loss-of-identity sense, but in the rhythm-of-life sense.

The phrases you've adopted.

The preferences you've shaped around each other.

The way you carry their memory through your day even when they're not near.

They're in your jokes.

In your plans.

In your quietest habits.

And none of it feels forced.

It just... *is.*

An integration.

A soft becoming.

The way a life folds around another without effort or expectation.

Closer than close isn't about being inseparable.

It's about being so secure in your connection that *separation isn't threatening.*

You can spend time apart.

You can miss each other without anxiety.

You can have full lives and still know: this bond is steady.

You don't need to be tethered to feel held.

You don't need to be in constant contact to feel considered.

There's a kind of freedom that comes with this closeness,

a shared breath that doesn't collapse under pressure.

It moves like trust.

It speaks like ease.

It *feels* like home.

You trust the quiet now.

You don't rush to fill every gap.

You don't misread pauses as problems.

You don't confuse a slow response for disinterest.

You've learned that presence isn't always loud,

sometimes it's just *available.*

And that availability, consistent, calm, caring,

has taught you that love doesn't always have to declare itself.

Sometimes it just shows up.

Sometimes it just stays.

Your conversations get deeper without needing to get heavier.

You talk about dreams without demanding timelines.

You ask real questions without turning them into interviews.

You say things like "I've been thinking..." and let the moment take shape on its own.

And they listen.

Not to solve.

Not to redirect.

But to know.

This is what closeness looks like when it's no longer chasing intimacy, but *living inside it*.

There's less tension now.

Not because you avoid conflict, but because you've built the muscle to move through it.

You don't explode.

You don't retreat.

You stay.

You say, "This felt off."

You say, "Can we talk about that?"

You say, "I want us to be good."

And they answer.

With care.

With curiosity.

With their own willingness to return.

Because now, you're not afraid of hard things.

You're only afraid of letting the hard things go unnamed.

You don't need constant reassurance anymore.

You still want tenderness, of course you do.

But the panic is gone.

You no longer treat love like something you might lose if you're not careful.

You've learned that love, the kind you've built now, doesn't vanish in silence.

It doesn't withdraw when you're tired.

It doesn't disappear when life gets messy.

It remains.

And that remaining has changed how you move.

You're softer now.

But somehow stronger too.

You're able to talk about the future, not as fantasy, not as pressure, but as curiosity.

You imagine things together.

You laugh about what could be.

You say things like, "I'd love that," and mean it, even if there's no immediate plan.

This is how closeness breathes:

By letting possibility in,

without needing certainty right away.

You're no longer building dreams to fix the present.

You're just letting the present expand to hold more hope.

You stop measuring closeness by intensity, and start measuring it by *consistency*.

Not how high the moments reach.

But how steady the ground feels beneath them.

It's not about fireworks.

It's about warmth.

A kind of emotional gravity that pulls you back to each other even after hard days.

And in that steadiness, something extraordinary happens:

You stop asking, "Are we okay?" every day.

Because you know you are.

Not perfectly.

Not effortlessly.

But *intentionally*.

There's a quiet joy in the way you begin to trust the ordinary.

You're no longer searching for grand signs.

You're no longer wondering if it's enough.

You wake up, exchange a few sleepy words, move through your morning, and something in you feels whole.

Because you're not chasing closeness anymore.

You're *living it*.

It doesn't have to declare itself.

It doesn't have to prove its presence.

It just *is*, folded into the fabric of your days.

You realize that the bond has become part of your inner world.

Not because you've lost yourself, but because their presence now exists in how you think, how you speak, how you care.

You catch yourself smiling at a memory mid-task.

You hear their voice in your head when you make a decision.

You soften in moments where you once would have closed off, because you've learned a different way of being.

They didn't change you.

But they *touched* something in you.

And now that touch lives on, even in your solitude.

You begin to protect the relationship differently.

Not with walls.

Not with fear.

But with intention.

You don't let resentment build.

You don't expect mind-reading.

You ask. You listen. You stay present.

Because this connection means something.

Not because it's rare, but because it's *real*.

And you know that real doesn't mean effortless.

It means *worth the effort*.

So you show up.

You speak clearly.

You choose them again, in the little ways that matter most.

You find rhythm in each other's lives.

The way your day starts.

The way you check in without needing a reason.

The way your bodies find each other in the middle of the night, even in sleep.

It's not about routine.

It's about resonance.

You're not syncing schedules, you're syncing *souls*.

There's room for individuality, yes.
But there's also a shared beat that you both feel.
A shared gravity you don't question.
This is what it means to move *with* someone,
not out of obligation, but out of ease.
You become less afraid of change.
Not because you expect things to stay the same,
but because you know how to adapt together.
You trust that whatever life brings, you'll keep showing up.
You'll keep adjusting.
You'll keep finding each other through the shifts.
You no longer grip tightly to the present out of fear.
You let it evolve.
You let it breathe.
Because you've built something that isn't afraid of time,
something that *moves with it.*
You don't ask for constant connection,
you ask for *honest* connection.
You don't need perfect communication,
you need real effort.
You don't need to be everything to each other,
you just need to be *true* to each other.
And that truth, spoken in quiet ways,
begins to feel like a kind of emotional home.
A place where you can bring your fullness,
your doubt, your joy, your fatigue,
and not feel like any of it is too much.
That's what makes closeness last.
Not intensity.
But acceptance.
You start to say things like,
"I'm tired today, but I'm here."
Or,

"I don't have much to say, but I still want to be near you."
And those moments mean more than any grand romantic gesture.
Because they say:
I still choose you, even when I don't feel like performing.
Even when life is quiet.
Even when I'm just... me.
That's the kind of love that becomes foundation.
The kind that doesn't crack when the mood shifts.
The kind that stays, gently,
even in the quietest hours.
There's a stillness in this kind of closeness.
A soft hum underneath everything.
A calm awareness that you're no longer trying to hold everything together alone.
You're not relying on them to fix your life.
But you are grateful to share it.
Grateful for the warmth of their presence beside you.
Grateful for the way they ask how your heart is doing, and wait for the real answer.
Grateful for the way you both make room for one another, without asking each other to shrink.
You've stopped needing to be perfect.
You've started learning how to be whole.
Together.
Eventually, you stop thinking of closeness as a goal.
It's no longer something you chase.
It's something you *notice*.
Something you *return to*.
Something you *live inside*.
You don't measure it by how often you talk, or how deeply you connect on any given day.
You feel it in the way they say your name.
In the way they remember the smallest things.

In the way they leave space when you need silence, not as distance, but as care.

Closeness becomes less about effort and more about presence.

Less about proving, more about *being*.

This kind of connection teaches you how to *rest*.

Not just in their arms, but in your life.

In your skin.

In your pace.

You're no longer rushing to feel secure.

You're no longer scanning for signs that they're pulling away.

You trust what's here.

You trust what's been built.

You trust the way they keep showing up, not perfectly, but steadily.

And that steadiness?

It frees you.

Not to disconnect,

but to *relax into belonging*.

You start to feel like yourself, not the version you once thought you had to be to keep someone close, but the *actual* version.

The one who gets quiet in the evenings.

The one who needs time alone to reset.

The one who cries over strange things and laughs at even stranger ones.

And they don't flinch.

They don't fix.

They don't fade.

They stay.

They witness.

They adjust.

Not to change you, but to *make room* for you.

And you do the same in return.

That's how closeness becomes real:

when it expands to fit *both of you fully*.

You begin to love differently.

Not harder.

Not louder.

Just *truer*.

You're no longer trying to avoid loss, you're simply focused on *showing up*.

You offer affection freely.

You express care without condition.

You let the small things mean what they mean, and let them matter.

You stop analyzing every exchange.

You start trusting the rhythm between you.

Because this is what trust has become:

a quiet certainty that you're on the same side,

even on hard days, even when words falter, even when life presses in.

You feel close even when you're not talking.

Even when they're in another room.

Even when the day is long and the to-do list is loud.

There's an invisible thread now,

a shared awareness.

A subtle comfort.

A presence that doesn't require attention to feel real.

It's not about proximity.

It's about *energy*.

The way their steadiness lives inside your nervous system.

The way your voice softens when you say their name.

The way you carry each other without even realizing you're doing it.

You understand now that love doesn't always feel electric.

Sometimes it feels like a warm bath.

Sometimes it feels like steady rain.

Sometimes it feels like the space you didn't know you needed until you exhaled inside it.

That's what closeness matures into.

Not less powerful, just less performative.

Not less meaningful, just more lived-in.

The kind of love you can lean on.

The kind of love you can laugh inside.
The kind of love you can *rest* in.
Because resting doesn't mean you're done,
it means you *trust what's here.*
There's a way you look at each other now, not searching, not questioning.
Just seeing.
Seeing the person they've become.
Seeing the effort they make.
Seeing the way they still care, even in the smallest, quietest ways.
You stop taking it for granted.
You stop expecting them to carry more than they should.
You meet them where they are, with appreciation, with patience, with your full self.
And in that mutual meeting, something rare happens:
Love becomes less about need, and more about *witnessing.*
And witnessing, at its core, is one of the deepest forms of connection.
This is the kind of closeness that feels like a rhythm.
Not a performance.
Not a pursuit.
A pattern you step into every day,
sometimes together, sometimes in your own space,
but always with the shared knowing:
We are here.
We are not what we once were.
We are not what we someday might be.
But we are *this.*
And that is enough.
Closeness like this doesn't always look profound from the outside.
It's the kind of connection that lives quietly.
In gestures.
In shared routines.
In the calm you feel even when they're not physically near.
And that quietness?

It's not emptiness, it's depth.

The kind of depth that doesn't demand to be seen to be real.

It's not performative.

It's not precious.

It's *present.*

Fully. Freely. Faithfully.

You start to notice how they've become part of your default emotional landscape.

When something good happens, you think of telling them first.

When something hard lands in your chest, you already feel the space they'll make for it.

When you're tired, you imagine how they'd hold the quiet with you, without needing to fix it.

They're not just someone you love.

They're someone your life now *includes.*

Not in a dependent way.

But in the way that trees grow near each other,

not tangled, but aware.

Not merged, but moved by each other's presence.

You stop needing to name the closeness every day.

You don't measure it by milestones.

You don't hold it to old expectations.

You just let it *exist.*

And that existence feels meaningful, even when it's simple.

You reach for their hand while walking and realize you didn't even think about it.

You make them tea without asking, because you already know which kind.

You sit beside them after a long day and don't feel the need to speak.

The silence is full.

The air is kind.

The moment is enough.

This is the kind of love that lives past the early spark.

It carries through seasons.

It weathers hard days.
It adapts.
It knows how to celebrate, and how to sit in the mundane.
It knows how to listen when words fall short.
It knows how to soften when life gets sharp.
It's not about recreating passion every day.
It's about cultivating peace.
It's about choosing *presence over performance*.
And when you have that,
you begin to understand what closeness truly means.
Closeness, real closeness, is about *trust in the ordinary*.
It's the peace you feel when nothing needs to be solved.
It's the grounding you return to without thinking.
It's the knowing that someone sees you, still, even when the world doesn't.
It's not a forever promise shouted from the rooftops.
It's a steady rhythm whispered between moments:
I'm still here.
You still matter.
We're still choosing this.
And eventually, you look around at your life and realize,
you're not chasing closeness anymore.
You've closed the distance.
You've lived through the stretch.
You've survived the silence.
You've returned, rebuilt, remained.
Now you're here, in the nearness you once dreamed of.
And it's not perfect.
But it's true.
You can feel it in your breath.
In your body.
In the way you show up, and the way they do too.
You no longer ask, "How do I hold on?"
You ask,

"How do I show up fully?"
"How do I love with softness?"
"How do I honor the space we've created?"
Because this space, this *closeness*, isn't a guarantee.
It's a garden.
And gardens need tending.
But it's no longer hard.
It's no longer heavy.
It's part of you now.
Natural.
Lived.
Felt.
Not fragile.
Not fleeting.
Fully here.
You made it.
Closer than close.
Closer than you ever thought possible.
And not because you tried harder,
but because you let yourself be seen.
You let them in.
You stayed when it was easier to run.
And now, what you share is not a firework.
It's a flame.
Sustainable.
Warming.
Quietly, beautifully alive.

About the Author

Toni Meli has always lived in the spaces between—between people and pauses, between the person you are and the one you're still becoming. As a triplet, they learned early how closeness can stretch and shape you, how it teaches you to listen closely even when nothing is being said.

At fourteen, Toni walked down a winding Pennsylvania road and into their first job at a winery—nervous, unsure, but willing. What began as a few hours among vines and barrels became years of steady work, quiet lessons, and unexpected growth. Now, at twenty-one, they help guide the heartbeat of that same place—managing the rhythm, holding the space for others, and noticing the beauty most people pass by.

Writing, for Toni, is just another way of paying attention. A way to hold what's fleeting. A way to reach across the quiet and say: *you're not alone.*

Closing the Distance is a piece of that journey—an offering from one life to another. A reminder that even in silence, something is being said. Even in distance, something is drawing us near.

Toni is the founder of Held Together Publishing and continues to live and work in Pennsylvania, finding depth in the familiar and wonder in the in-between.

Author photograph by - Zach Erwin (zerwinmedia.com)

www.ingramcontent.com/pod-product-compliance
Lightning Source LLC
Chambersburg PA
CBHW062104080426

42734CB00012B/2746